Psalm Stories

Liz Petty

ISBN:9780578900308

Cover design by Amanda McWhirter
Licensor's Author: Jcomp – Freepik.com
Library of Congress Control Number: 0578900297

To Josh –

My support, my sanity, my steady

You are my best friend and my favorite

PSALM STORIES

CONTENTS

*DAY NUMBER CORRESPONDS TO PSALM CHAPTERS

PSALM STORIES

PREFACE

In 2019 I felt the Lord tell me to read through the book of Psalms and jot down one verse from each chapter that really spoke to me. So, I began to read one chapter a day and do just that.

Months later after joining a writing community, Hope*Writers, I began to think about my story and what I wanted to share with others. How could I connect and share what He shared with me?

It's like He tapped me on the shoulder and showed me the journal I had started. That journal has now turned into this, "Psalm Stories."

"Psalm Stories" was written as if you and I were sitting having coffee and some kind of delicious chocolate discussing the verses. I am no Biblical scholar. I am no preacher. I'm just a passionate human who continues to learn about the unending amount of grace that God extends to every one of us. I've believed a lot of lies about Him and He has so gently peeled those lies off and revealed truths. I hope to show those truths with you through these words.

This book is designed to be used alongside you as you read the chapters of the book of Psalms. While the individual verses I use from each chapter are powerful, you will understand more if you read the full chapter along with the day's writing. Most of the daily passages end with a reflecting question and a prayer. I encourage you to dwell on those and come back to them as needed.

I hope you feel seen and known and fully loved by the God that made you and is consistently pursuing you with unending grace.

Thank you for reading alongside with me.

- Liz

PSALM STORIES

DAY 1

"That person is like a tree planted by streams of water which yields fruit in season and whose leaf does not wither - whatever they do prospers." Psalm 1:3

It is fitting to me that the first day mentions trees. It is one of the clearest ways I see Him. The detail. The strength. The quiet beauty. This is what I hope to be, planted by water, always prospering as the tree David describes.

That would be nice right? Knowing whatever you attempt is going to prosper and be successful. I don't know about you, but that's not how my life has always been. I've either tried and failed a few times, or (lots of times) sat on the side, procrastinated and not tried for fear of not prospering.

The very beginning of the book of Psalms encourages us to not be in step with the wicked or sit in the company of mockers. (vs. 1) It goes on to say that those who delight in the law of the Lord and meditate on it day and night are blessed. So often we turn from the law of the Lord and instead turn toward something with instant validation - receiving short lived acceptance from others.

I never enjoy the phrase the 'law of the Lord' as it portrays a mean, disconnected, judge. Something limited. It seems non-accepting. That's definitely not something I want to spend all day thinking about. It's easier to give in to quick fixes and 'acceptance' from others.

But if I think of 'the law of the Lord' as instruction, guidance, advice, etc. and relate it to my 'law' in my classroom or at home…then that I can understand. Any instruction or law that I give to my students and children is always for their benefit. They may not understand it. They may not like it. But I never ask them to follow something that is not for their prosperity. It's the same with His law.

Also, His law, the Word, is not just a set of rules. It's one big redemption love story. It's His calling out to us to restore broken fellowship. It's a reminder of truths that set us free.

Today, may your delight and meditation be on Him and His promises. Keep your roots grounded in His life-giving water, keep your thoughts on His voice, His guidance and direction, then your leaves will not wither and will prosper.

Praying your roots find His water today.

DAY 2

"Blessed are all who take refuge in Him." Psalm 2:12b

Refuge - safety, protection, a break from running and fretting and worrying

Are you quick to turn to Him for refuge and accept the safety, protection and break that He offers? I believe sometimes we are afraid to admit we need help, afraid that if someone saw how bad it really is then they would no longer offer help. Some of us would rather continue to carry the heavy burden instead of admitting how much of a strain it has become, afraid someone may shame us.

Sometimes I put off seeking refuge with Him because it honestly wouldn't feel like a break, it would feel like a chore, more tap dancing. There are times my burden is too heavy that there is no energy left to tap dance in order to retrieve my rest and help.

And that is the problem. When we go to Him with that mindset of "if I spend "x" amount of time with Him, read "x" amount of the Bible, then He will be pleased with my effort and grant me refuge."

Listen. That is <u>not</u> how He is. There is NO amount of time nor number of chapters to read in the Bible, there is no amount of selfless giving you could undertake to earn His refuge. *He simply gives it.*

It is a mindset we must change. He knows the burdens we carry. We don't have to carry them all the way to a designated spot in order for Him to take them from us. He is with you wherever you go.

Why not ask Him right where you are, right now, in the middle of the chest tightening worry, in the middle of the giant mess in your home, through the loud chaos of children fighting again? Ask Him for refuge. He's there. He'll give it. You will be blessed.

Praying refuge and blessing for you today.

DAY 3

"But You, Lord, are a shield around me, my glory, the One who lifts my head high." Psalm 3:3

This world is constantly giving us reasons to feel shame. Body image, relationship status, grades, social media standards. I worry constantly that who I think I am may just be a farce and others know the real truth and just won't tell me. That I walk in a confidence that shouldn't be. Some of us feel shame when we think about His perspective of us. It is so hard for us to understand that He tips our chin up to look at Him to see Him smile at us.

It is He who is our glory. It is He who is our shield against the lies from the world and our own head. It is He who lifts our heads high. He wants you to raise your head to accept all that He says you are. You are a conqueror. You are precious. You are a friend of Jesus, not a slave. He has taken away all shame.

Some of you may find that very hard to accept. But answer this, is it possible for Him to lie? It's not. So, when He says He calls you friend, loved one, precious in His sight know that it is true.

Where are you hanging your head in shame? What lies are you believing? Do not allow lies to keep your head down in shame anymore. Look up. Claim His truth about you and let Him lift your head high.

Praying for truth to be louder than lies for you today.

DAY 4

"How long will you people turn my glory into shame? Know that the Lord has set apart His faithful servant for Himself." Psalm 4:2-3

Psalm 3:3 states that the Lord is our glory. Here David asks how long will glory be turned to shame.

How many times have we been shown our calling, our glory, but shame has stopped us from fully stepping out into it? When will we realize that He did not create and rescue us just as a trophy, something to keep on a shelf? We are created in His image and since Eden, He has given us *partnership*, a role, a responsibility in naming, caring for and continuing His creation. These callings are shown in hundreds of different ways. Some of us are called to help maintain order, caretake, create, find beauty, research, explore, lead, make peace.

It is one thing to begin to hold up our heads and begin to believe what He says about us. It's another to walk in that belief unashamed.

You doing what you were created to do isn't self-serving, self-promoting or egotistical. It is taking the shame off His glory. It is being responsible of the talents He's given you, trusting Him with steps of faith and freedom to do what you were put here to do. You have been set apart for Him, not as a slave, but as a friend, a child, an heir that has a special role that *only you can fill.*

Where is shame stopping you? Where is fear hindering you? It's time to stop turning His glory into shame.

Praying you take a bold, brave step into His calling of glory today.

DAY 5

"But I, by Your great love, can come into Your house; in reverence I bow down toward Your holy temple." Psalm 5:7

We have heard that He stands at the door of our hearts asking to come in. Here we see not only does He wish to have access to our homes, our hearts, but we are allowed to go into His. Invited guests. You. Me. All of us. An invitation to be with Him in His home, His comfort place, His dwelling.

Homes are another layer of deeper intimacy. He is not a god that does not grant you access behind the curtain. He literally ripped the curtain in half and invited you in. (Matthew 27:51) We have access to all He has.

It does not say, 'but I, by obligation, by guilt, by resentment, can come into Your house.' No. It says by love. Take a second and let it sink in that the Creator, the King invites you into His house today out of love. He. Wants. You. There.

Are there things you are searching for in your own home, your own heart, that you cannot find? Desires? Needs? Hopes? Strength? Have you checked His house? I'm sure He has it there. You're invited in. Verse 11 states, "let all who take refuge in You be glad; let them ever sing for joy." I imagine you could ask Him for whatever it is you're looking for and He would help you find it there in His house, in His heart.

Praying that you find yourself boldly crossing the threshold into His home today.

DAY 6

"The Lord has heard my weeping. The Lord has heard my cry for mercy; the Lord accepts my prayer." Psalm 6:8-9

Your cries are not silent to God. He hears your weeping. He hears you beg for mercy for your situation.

And not only does He hear you. He accepts your prayer - your long and rambling prayer, your quick prayer with no formal opening or closing or following a step-by-step guide, your carefully thought-out prayer, your prayer you utter while falling asleep and the morning fog prayer with gunk still in your eyes. He accepts the prayers you think He doesn't hear, the ones you think are trivial. "Why am I even praying this? He's got much bigger things to tend to." Nope. He hears and accepts those, too. He even accepts the prayers that are so raw, so angry. The prayers when crying for mercy is mingled with rage and confusion, the ones you can't believe you just thought. He accepts them.

A synonym for accepts is welcomes. He welcomes whatever it is you have to give Him. Questions, weeping, gratitude, rage. He's not scared by your thoughts or emotions. He accepts them. He welcomes them.

Praying you find vulnerability to share your heart's cry with Him today.

DAY 7

"My shield is God Most High who saves the upright in heart."
Psalm 7:10

Shield - defense, support, shelter, protection from close range or projectiles.

How comforting to know God does not expect you to "get through the battle" and then come to Him. Not only is He *with* you on the field in the middle of it, but *He is also your shield.*

He took all the hits for you. He protects from close range, up close and personal blows and those from far off. Those you tried to prepare for and still managed to find you.

I've spent a lot of my life in prevention mode. "If I do x,y, and z, then that will prevent such and such from happening." I put my shield down and tried to calculate the best footing to avoid all blows. Not possible. Not wise.

It's not a question of *if* attacks will come, it's when. Why tire yourself and depend on your own wisdom and strength when He offers Himself as your shield?

Where do you need to pick up your Shield and allow Him to protect you from the current and future attacks? How can you let Him be your defender instead of you trying to do it all by yourself?

Praying you feel His loving, powerful protection over you today.

DAY 8

"Through the praise of children and infants You have established a stronghold against Your enemies to silence the foe and the avenger." Psalm 8:2

I had the opportunity to worship alongside one of these very children mentioned in this verse. She stood on top of her chair boldly singing the songs. Her praise was loud, sometimes off key, her arms were flailing. At times she would throw out a "hallelujah." At first it was distracting, but quickly it was obvious she was a vessel of His glory and it was truly glorious. It was an honor to worship alongside her. She was brave, unashamed and full of hope. She made me see Him clearer, hear Him more distinctly. She encouraged me to focus on Him. My doubts, troubles, enemies seemed to silence as she encouraged me and helped me to focus on Him.

How often do we hinder our praise because of shame, fear, doubt? There have been many times I quieted my voice, stilled my body, sat down or stood up just to fit in. Many of us feel we are unqualified to praise or worship. A child, an infant cannot truly even sing the words on the screen. But they do sing out the utterances of their hearts. It is not about qualification. Those children and infants who have no 'qualifications' are the ones He uses to establish a stronghold against enemies. Praising like a child - loud, messy, unashamed, innocent, full of Him, His love, His power, His glory, His delight - is where foes are silenced. Being strong in your love of Him establishes a stronghold against enemies.

I encourage you to remember that praise and worship isn't just a 20-minute set before a sermon filled with singing. Worship is praising Him - through your words, your movements, your attentiveness, your resting, your encouragement, your preparation, your stillness, your noise with all your focus on Him. That is praise.

Where can you be more like a child in your praise?

Praying you release yourself of the need for control in order to be fully abandoned by praise for Him today.

DAY 9

"Those who know Your name trust in You, for You, Lord, have never forsaken those who seek You." Psalm 9:10

Those who know His name trust in Him. It's hard to imagine a culture where someone has never heard of God or of Jesus. Those places exist. There are also places that have heard the name, but don't know the name.

Emmanuel, Yahweh, Prince of Peace, Abba, I Am, El Roi, Jehovah, there are countless names of the Father. I love how names in the Bible have such significance and meaning, and His names are just the same. And in each of those names we learn of new ways to trust Him.

When we learn of Him and learn of His character through different names, God with us, the Lord, Papa, the God who sees, we learn new areas in which to trust Him. I believe He has many different names for the many different seasons we all have in our lives. For each one, He has a different name, a different way of showing up for you there. Some seasons you may relate to Him more as Abba, some as El Roi, or you may have one constant such as Emmanuel that takes you through them all.

Regardless of which name you call, His is the greatest and most powerful name and you can trust it. If you call to Him, He will meet you there. You have His word. He will not forsake you.

How can you seek out His name in your current situation? Where do you need to learn to trust Him more fully?

Praying He shows you more and more of His incredible strengths through His name today.

DAY 10

"You, Lord, hear the desire of the afflicted; You encourage them and You listen to their cry." Psalm 10:17

Have you felt afflicted? How about troubled, bothered, irritated? Those seem like more relatable terms to me. We do not have to suppress those before we go to God. He already hears those troubles. When you bring them to Him, in all your bothered, frustrated, confused, angry state, just as you are, you then give Him the opportunity to encourage you. Not fix, not berate, not tsk tsk, but to encourage you and listen to you.

He listens to your cry. Not with an eye roll. Not with an exasperated 'would you hush about it already?!?' God simply listens. Take heart in that. He listens and encourages.

Can you take that frustration to Him? (Even if it might be about Him?) Can you trust He's big enough to take it and wants to encourage and listen to you?

Praying you will find full freedom to be your true self with Him right now and let Him in just to simply be there.

DAY 11

"For the Lord is righteous, He loves justice; the upright will see His face." Psalm 11:17

The upright. To be honest that feels like a 'works' mentality with which I honestly have struggles. I do not believe there is anything we can or cannot do works wise that will give us access to see God's face.

The earlier verses in this chapter talk of the foundations being destroyed. When my foundations have been destroyed, I've been face down not upright. Everything turned upside down, not knowing what to believe anymore. There were many many times I refused to hope, refused to look. It was more comfortable and less painful to keep my face down. The mere thought of facing up, turning over to look at the new reality was too challenging and excruciating.

But eventually, I learned to slowly turn my face away from my pillow, slowly turn and dare to look upright.

When I think of upright in that context, not perfect, not works based, *but an attitude of turning and facing* that which scares me, angers me, worries me most and looking at it, maybe not even head on, but one slow shift at a time, when I turn to look for Him, I do…I see His face.

Praying for you to find the strength and courage to begin to turn from your despair to see He is there. Praying He begins to show you more and more of His beautiful face.

DAY 12

"Help, Lord, for no one is faithful anymore; those who are loyal have vanished from the human race." Psalm 12:1

We have all felt this before. Betrayed. Alone. Duped. We humans are a fickle bunch. We "lie to our neighbors and flatter them with our lips, but harbor deception in our hearts." (vs. 2) There is definitely power of life and death in the tongue. What we say matters. What we hear from others matters. Greatly.

However, we must remember to hold the words of ourselves and others up against God's great truth. "The words of the Lord are flawless, like silver purified in a crucible, like gold refined seven times." (vs. 6)

It is so easy to build our worth, security and truth on what this world says. What our coworkers say, what the observation sheet says, the test results, the social media notifications. We wait on others to tell us what we want and need to hear before we believe it for ourselves. And then when those voices silence or turn negative we find ourselves doubting all that was previously said.

What if we remember He has the final word? "Because the poor are plundered and the needy groan, I will now arise," says the Lord. "I will protect them from those who malign them."' (vs. 5)

What words and beliefs do you need to give Him and ask Him to show you the truth versus the lies? What part of your heart needs His words and His truth?

Praying for Him to show you lies you've believed and truth you've been hesitant to accept.

DAY 13

"But I trust in Your unfailing love; my heart rejoices in Your salvation. I will sing the Lord's praise, for He has been good to me."
Psalm 13:5-6

This is David's response to his own plea, "How long, Lord? Will you forget me forever? How long will you hide Your face from me? How long must I wrestle with my thoughts and day after day have sorrow in my heart? How long will my enemy triumph over me?" (vs. 1-2)

But I will trust, rejoice and sing. Because He has been good…to me.

In the midst of your despair may you remember He is good not just in general, not just to others, not just as a personality attribute, but He is good to you.

It is easy to trust, rejoice and sing when things are easy, and life seems stable. But on those days when we can't even find His face to look at Him, when we question what we thought He told us, when we wrestle with our thoughts and have sorrows in our hearts, in the very midst of the enemy triumphing over us may we still say we trust His unfailing love and still sing how He is good to us.

Can we still cry out to Him in the middle of the hurt and then take it one step further and declare trust? Are we willing to still sing of His goodness in the middle of an ongoing battle?

Praying for you today to find the strength to acknowledge the hurt and still trust, rejoice and sing of His goodness to you.

DAY 14

"...God is present in the company of the righteous." Psalm 14:5

Righteous is not my favorite term. It seems too unattainable. Sometimes it gives me anxiety just thinking about all I've done to mess up righteousness.

I believe this chapter is stating that anyone that *seeks* Him is righteous. Those who are considered righteous are the ones who have His presence with and around them. And that makes sense. If I go and hang around Krispy Kreme, then I'm gonna smell like Krispy Kreme. When my son spends time outside, he ends up coming in smelling like the outdoors. *You can't help but take on the characteristics of the presence in which you enter.*

Therefore, if I seek Him, He is there. And if He is there, His righteousness is greater and denser a fog than that of the freshest of donuts. And because of that, it makes me righteous. If I am considered righteous, which I am, He is *with* me in any and all situations. Therefore, I have nothing to dread or fear.

Is there an area in which you are fearful, dreadful? You are righteous if you are with Him. And if you ask, He's there.

Praying for Him to show you His presence and righteousness today and because of that bring you peace that you have nothing to fear or dread.

DAY 15

"Lord, who may dwell in Your sacred tent?...the one who speaks the truth from their heart." Psalm 15:1-2

Somewhere along the line Christianity has gotten this wrong. Some seem to believe that in order to dwell with Him, you must always tell the truth no matter who is offended or hurt. That boldly speaking truth with no regard to whom you're speaking will keep you in 'good graces' with Him, keep you dwelling in His presence. They seem to take no regard to their own heart or the heart of others. Then there are others who only pay attention to the heart, oftentimes foregoing important truth in order to spare the heart any unease.

It has taken me many, many long years to even begin to learn how to balance this. Jesus told people difficult things. He always spoke truth and He always spoke them out of love with everyone's hearts in mind. But a lot of times what He said disrupted people. It shocked some. It made some people angry. Sometimes truth and His relaying of that truth even made Him angry. Being like Jesus doesn't mean only pointing out truths and sins.

Being like Jesus also doesn't mean always making sure people are comfortable no matter what.

The fact is the truth is in disruption. If it ever becomes too comfortable, we can be assured that we've gotten accustomed to the broken patterns of this world. He comes to set things right again. He *is* truth. Sometimes it's uncomfortable, but it's never accusatory or mean spirited. He longs for truth to set all things right again.

Where do you need to speak the truth even if it may cause some disruption in your life? Where do you need to consider the heart behind the what and the why of the specific truths you are speaking and ensure you are taking hearts into account? Where do you think He is lovingly speaking truth over you? Do you see Him as only heart without truth? Or only truth without heart?

Praying you know deep down in your bones any hard truths He may have for you are coming to you from such a large heart that is relentless about setting yours right again, even if it may hurt for a little while.

DAY 16

"The boundary lines have fallen for me in pleasant places; surely I have a delightful inheritance." Psalm 16:6

Boundaries - the separation of different units, identities, a clear marking

Throughout the Old Testament we read of the importance of land. It was a symbol of a community. It was their identity. There were walls that marked where one area began and one ended. Boundaries.

Growing up I knew little of boundaries. In an effort to feel included and seen, there were few boundaries in my home. Sometimes this is just as damaging as never letting anyone in. When you lose boundaries, you lose yourself. You merge so homogeneously that your own identity goes missing.

I know of some who grew up with countless boundaries. They knew no freedom. Intimacy of any kind was foreign to them. They adapted a "no one comes in and no one gets hurt" mentality.

Like most all things, there must be a balance. Boundaries are a 'delightful inheritance.' They allow a distinct sense of self in order to maintain health and they allow community and intimacy. We are not meant to do this life alone. Nor are we meant to never guard ourselves. Jesus has boundaries. Let me repeat that. Jesus has boundaries. There were some people that did not receive healing. Why did He limit His disciples to 12? Why did only a handful go with Him to the garden? Why did *He* often steal away from some alone time? Boundaries.

Do you have boundary lines that need to be adjusted to 'pleasant places?' Would it help you to widen your boundaries and let some people in? Do you need to construct some clear boundary lines for yourself and allow yourself some health and balance?

Praying that He will show you how to balance all of the boundary lines in this life so that you may experience your delightful inheritance.

DAY 17

"Show me the wonders of You great love, You who save by Your right hand those who take refuge in You from their foes."
Psalm 17:7

Show me the wonders of Your great love. Show me the hidden things. Show me the beauty of Your love.

This walk, this relationship with God - yes, we are called to trust even when it's hard and it seems impossible to see His love, let alone the wonders of His great love. But here we see David out right demand to see the wonders of His great love. Not the obligation or the 'regular,' but the surprising, beautiful, unexpected type of great love.

He spent the first few verses of this chapter begging for Him to hear and respond. Now he demands for God to show up and show off His love.

Understand that God knows your unsaid thoughts, your hidden doubts. It is not an outlandish request for us to ask Him to show us His great love. He is not offended by this. I believe He kindly just wipes the fog away from our glasses so we can see more clearly - His wondrous great love has been around this whole time. It has never left. And He has no problem wiping away that which blocks our view.

The underlying point in these verses - He not only saves, but He also shows the wonders of great love.

Where could you ask for a clearer picture of His great love? Have you sought refuge in Him, even in your doubts? Take them to Him. He will save you from your foes and show His great love for you.

Praying you will take it all to Him and remember He came not just to save us from the results of the fallen world, but also to live abundantly with His great love in clear view.

DAY 18

"In my distress I called to the Lord; I cried to my God for help. From His temple He heard my voice." Psalm 18:6

David sang this psalm after being delivered from his enemies. Be comforted. Like David, if you are in the middle of distress, cords of death entangling you, torrents of destruction overwhelming you (vs. 4), cry out to your God for help. Even if you feel you are outside God's temple, far from Him, He hears your voice. Not only that, but He knows and recognizes your voice. He knows your voice from all others. It doesn't matter if you pray a 'fancy' prayer or just simply cry out, He hears you.

"From His temple, He heard my voice." Remember because the curtain ripped in two, even if you feel far away you are never not in His temple. As soon as you call to Him, you are right there with Him. Do not believe the lie that you are ever out of earshot from Him.

Is there any desire or concern, frustration, any expression that you've held within, believing He wouldn't hear it anyway?

Praying you will find the courage to voice your heart to Him and find comfort knowing that He recognizes even your smallest whisper. I encourage you to utter to Him right now and then finish reading all of this chapter to see how intentionally He comes to us when we call.

DAY 19

"The heavens declare the glory of God; the skies proclaim the work of His hands." Psalm 19:1

We can try, but it's not possible to put God in a box. We miss so many chances to see and hear Him, to experience His glory when we think He only shows up in a specific building on specific days at specific times in specific ways.

It took me a while to realize I'm not crazy for experiencing Him in nontraditional ways. I used to stare at clouds and be in complete awe. I'd see Him there. He's spoken to me in music, nature, even through one of the kids' cartoon shows (now that's a great story!) He is personal and speaks to each of His children in a special personal way.

The heavens declare the glory of God. I believe when we are finally with Him fully, we will be blown away at how many messages He leaves for us every second. We just have to learn the language and adjust our seeing. David says the sun is like a bridegroom (Jesus) and nothing is deprived of its warmth. (vs. 4-6) Think of what the sunlight, Jesus, touches. Everything. Nothing is deprived of Him. His message of love to you is all around.

How have you experienced Him in nontraditional ways? Where do you think He may be leaving you messages of His love and declarations of His glory? Share those ways with others so they may look for God there as well!

Praying for you to be able to sense, feel, see and hear Him in many new ways, Take a step of faith and dare to believe that He is speaking to you even if you feel crazy. Praying you feel the warmth of the Bridegroom Sun today.

DAY 20

"Some trust in chariots and some in horses, but we trust in the name of the Lord our God. They are brought to their knees, and fall, but we rise up and stand firm." Psalm 20:7-8

Those who trust in chariots and horses are brought to their knees and fall. The ones who trust the things of this world - the way things have always been done, the latest and greatest new ideas, new revolutionary products to change their lives, old tried and true methods that are guaranteed to fill all their deep needs, are eventually going to be let down.

My chariots and horses look a lot like codependent relationships and perfectionism. Me depending on me and how I can function just right to ensure love, validation and security. The 'sureness' of someone else's love and me making sure to never rock the boat. It may have taken me a few decades to fully understand, but those ways of doing life bring me to my knees and cause me to fail. My guidelines. My rule books that I made up. My flimsy net of security that I knitted with one codependent lie after another.

After lots of therapy, understanding, and failed attempts, I'm slowly and surely learning that *the only way to rise up and stand firm is to trust in Him.* He doesn't change. His rule book has already been checked off and signed as completed. He is not codependent or manipulative.

What are your chariots and horses? What do you find yourself trusting in and then wondering why you've fallen on your knees?

Praying for you to learn how to lean on Him instead of your own understanding a little more today. Praying your knees begin to straighten and your feet feel firm ground underneath you as He helps to raise you up.

DAY 21

"Surely You have granted him unending blessings and made him glad with the joy of Your presence." Psalm 21:6

Unending blessings with the joy of His presence. There are times it may seem like the blessings may have dried up, disappeared. The idea of having joy may seem like a mystery to you. I've been there. Angry at God, no joy, feeling alone, bitter, hurt and confused.

David does not equate *happiness* with His presence, but *joy.* Joy is a choice. Joy does not equal happy or put together. It's a mindset, a deliberate choosing of triumphant thinking and awareness of God's presence, His presence that brings true joy.

He doesn't guarantee smooth sailing - He guarantees His presence with us in the boat. When we know He is with us, it is still ok to feel whatever we need to feel, just know those feelings do not have the final say. The next time your life is feeling tumultuous, upside down, far from hashtag blessed and joyful, try to make a conscious effort to become aware of His presence. That's where the unending blessings are. That's where the joy resides.

Do you have an example of choosing joy amid chaos in your life? Share it with someone!

Praying for the awareness of His presence to overcome you with full deliberate joy today.

DAY 22

"From You comes the theme of my praise in the great assembly." Psalm 22:25

The theme of our praises revolves around God. There has been some debate about whether or not we should praise Him for small details, a good parking spot, a good hair day, a found $20 in a coat pocket. While I don't believe that our relationship with Him is only to get 'trivial' blessings or that He is waiting on a thank you for every tiny little thing, I do believe that He is in every facet of our life. In all honesty, we have no idea of the countless amounts of reasons to praise at any given moment. So, if parking spots, good hair days, found $20 bring you joy, wholeness, peace, or awareness of His presence, praise Him for it.

I believe what David is saying here is in anything we have to praise, it comes from Him. He is in every good thing. When you see Him in it, let Him know.

Have you noticed even a tiny reason to praise Him recently? Share it with someone!

Praying for you to see Him so clearly and be able to praise His presence privately or publicly.

DAY 23

"The Lord is my Shepherd, I lack nothing." Psalm 23:1

For years I've read this verse through the eyes of material possessions. I'll never have to worry about shelter or food. While this is true, I'm also learning that it means much more.

I lack nothing. Through our Shepherd I'm never not enough. Through my marriage, my parenting, my job, friendships, passions, duties…I lack nothing. When He is my Shepherd, I am enough.

Phrases such as, "I'm not good enough, pretty enough, quiet enough, loud enough, thin enough, fit enough, experienced enough, pure enough, clean enough, polished enough" dissolve when we realize that with Him We. Lack. Nothing.

NOTHING. Do you hear me? Every single thing you feel like you need to accomplish before you achieve validation, success, the right to rest, approval, whatever your heart has been searching for…wait no longer. With. Him. You. Lack. Nothing.

What have you been holding out on, beating yourself up over, striving so hard to grasp? What one more step are you waiting to happen before you can move on in rejoicing and resting like the remainder of Psalm 23 depicts? Where do you think you lack? Let Him show you that you *already have it.*

Praying you find the joy in this truth today. May you walk in the freedom of lacking no thing. You. Are. Enough. Woo y'all!

Let our eyes be open! Let us rest, walk, and run in this freedom He gives!

DAY 24

"Who is the King of glory? The Lord strong and mighty, the Lord mighty in battle." Psalm 24:8

In Psalm 23 we see David describe the Lord as a shepherd, leading, guiding, comforting. Here in the next chapter, he describes Him as strong, mighty and in battle.

What seems at first glance to be a contradiction is really an important combination. He is gentle and comforting all while also being strong and mighty. Mighty in battle. In a fight. In a big ole confrontation. Somewhere along the line we've believed things must be in one group or the other. This person straight up tells it like it is and dares anyone to say otherwise. While another person is a big ole softie of a heart. One will let you get away with murder and one will be as aggressive as a mama bear. Which one is He? Which one is best? Both. Shepherding, comforting and guiding is as equally important as strength and might. As long as they are both done in love, they are both capable of showing His character and glory.

It's taken me a while to grasp this. The beauty in both, the importance and necessity of both. We are not called to just be guiding and comforting. Nor does He only come to us with aggression and war on His mind. The true power is in the balance. It's not that we love to fight. We fight to love. It's what He shows us. The King of glory, the Lord mighty in battle, the Lord our Shepherd.

Do you find yourself on one side or the other? Do you view Him as only Shepherd or Warrior?

I'm praying that today you begin to see both sides of Him and know that both come from a place of agape love.

DAY 25

"He will instruct them in the ways they should choose."
Psalm 25:12

I feel most of us would acknowledge that we want to do His will. The question that usually follows is, "What *is* His will?"

Many of us spend so much time wondering and wringing hands over that answer. Some of us take off in one direction blazing paths that maybe weren't on our maps.

The Israelites got themselves wandering through the desert for decades. But He led them with a pillar of fire and a pillar of cloud. When it moved, they moved. When it stopped, they stopped. Sometimes He gives a specific direction, a definitive answer. Sometimes He keeps the pillar of fire and smoke hovering in the same spot, and we make camp and keep our eyes on Him to give us the way we should choose.

Are you waiting on instruction from Him on which way to choose? Can you see Him, but He's had you make camp while you wait on Him to show you the next steps?

Praying for you to be able to see Him in the fire, in the cloud, in the stillness. He will instruct you. Go listen.

DAY 26

"Lord, I love the house where You live, the place where Your glory dwells." Psalm 26:8

Eden, the ark of the covenant, the temple, all of these are places where God's presence was known, felt, alive. I cannot imagine living in a time where His house was a specific temple or finite place. How fortunate we are to live in post-curtain time. A time when His presence continues to flow out between the ripped curtain that once separated us.

How precious a thought, the God who once walked among the garden with His creations, still managed to find a way to be around us after the fall. He who is set apart did not cast us out of the garden to suffer alone but gave great thought to the details of a man-made ark and temple. A pigeonhole of a structure to try to fit His glory into and protect it from the effects of the fallen world. He so desperately wanted to be with His people.

How precious a thought that once it became obvious the small abode would no longer contain His Glory and Love of His children, He Himself made it possible to tear that curtain right in half, declaring any that would, could find themselves in His presence.

Lord, I love the house where You live, the place where Your glory dwells. Don't you see? He stooped. He tore. He bent. In order for Him to still be able to be with you. His glory is all around you. His peaceful, joyful, understanding, all powerful presence is accessible to you right this very second.

What may be blocking you from recognizing His presence in the day-to-day moments? How incredible that He couldn't get enough of us and made sure we could fellowship again now and forever?

Praying that in the midst of busy days, we all will remember, recognize and experience the presence of Him around us today.

DAY 27

"For in the day of trouble He will keep me safe in His dwelling; He will hide me in the shelter of His sacred tent and set me high upon a rock." Psalm 27:5

Sometimes when you feel as if you're hidden, not seen, it is actually Him hiding you to protect you.

Sometimes the darkness that frightens is actually the shadow of His wing covering you.

His sacred tent is His presence. Therefore, take heart, in the day of trouble He hides you in His presence. (verse 5)

Some of us feel that in days of trouble it's our job and expectation to be out on the battlefield. Have you thought that sometimes you are meant to be hidden in His presence? Let Him fight.

Where are you feeling unseen? Invisible? In the dark? Ask Him to show you which parts of that hiddenness is His protection over you.

Praying you find comfort in the unseen and in the darkness knowing even in those times, He finds a way to bring comfort, protection and love.

DAY 28

"The Lord is my strength and my shield; my heart trusts in Him and He helps me. My heart leaps for joy, and with my song I praise Him." Psalm 28:7

Whether you're a teacher, a student or parent to a school age child most of us know the grind of school. The mornings of leaping out of bed in a rush or savoring the last few minutes willing yourself to get out and get going. The juggling of schedules and trying to remember what's been checked off the never ending to do list for multiple events for possibly multiple children at multiple schools. The emotions are stirred by awards days, birthdays, holidays, symbolic steps of precious time fleeing from us faster than we imagined, trying to savor the moment and be present while fighting off the countless reminders running through our heads. We. Need. Help.

And He reminds us none of this mania is ours to carry alone. He is our strength. When we feel we can't deal with one more thing, He does. When we feel attacked by more reminders and sentimental passings, He is our shield. Through that we can learn to trust Him. And though our bones are tired, are backs are sore and our hearts feel they've been through an extra rinse and spin cycle, they can leap for joy. We can find a song of praise…even if it's a very tired and out of tune melody.

Where can you let Him provide strength for you? Where can you still find joy at the end of crowded weeks?

Praying *rest* for you. Praying His strength finds you. Praying you find joy all around.

DAY 29

"The voice of the Lord is powerful; the voice of the Lord is majestic." Psalm 29:4

The voice of the Lord. He speaks.

God is not a passive God only wanting us to herald Him while He remains silent. **He responds.**

His words are intentional, full of a strength and power we cannot comprehend. He encourages.

He calls light out of darkness, land out of sea, flesh out of dust. He creates.

He rejoices over you with song. He sings.

His voice calls kings out of shepherds, blesses buffets out of baskets, and redeems His children out of bondage. He renews.

His voice is gentle, not weak; strong, not scary; majestic, not insecure and He uses it to invite us into His glory.

What is His voice saying to you today?

Praying you overwhelmingly hear Him and His message today.

DAY 30

"You turned my wailing into dancing; You removed my sackcloth and clothed me with joy, that my heart may sing Your praises and not be silent." Psalm 30:11-12

Our God is a God who is burdened for us. He does not want us to suffer. But that is not all. He does more than remove the wailing and the sackcloth. He does not simply want the wailing to stop, He replaces it with dancing. He does not leave us unclothed after removing the sackcloth. He clothes us in joy!

There is so much more to His will for us than simply removing the bad. He does not *just* defeat death; He comes to bring life and life abundantly! He provides us the freedom to dance in joy! Take heart! Your wailing will one day end. Your tattered clothes will be replaced. And He will bring you to more of Him and His glory!

He wants our hearts to sing and not be silent. There is no shame in sharing His beauty. Sometimes our praises are stifled by those still in sackcloth. They can't understand our dancing. That's ok. Your singing heart reminds them there is more and may encourage them to turn their attention to the One who trades our sackcloth for joy.

Are you burdened right now with endless wailing waiting desperately for relief? Or have you been sitting without wailing, but not sure how to get up and dance? Not sure if it's ok to be happy and joyful in your current season?

I pray you allow yourself to come alive to Joy once your season of wailing is over. Get ready. Your dancing days will soon be here.

DAY 31

"I will be glad and rejoice in Your love, for You saw my affliction and knew the anguish of my soul. You have not given me into the hands of my enemy but have set my feet in a spacious place."
Psalm 31:7-8

Why is it that when we are in seasons of rest and abundance, a harvest, that we are hesitant to show JOY? Like true, exhale, honest to goodness, "I can relax now," Joy. I know for me I grew up in a constant state of prevention mode. Always on the lookout for the next stormy season and being sure we were all prepared for it. That's exhausting.

The rain has an important role. The hard times make us push up through that ground so that we may fully be who He made us to be. Those times are necessary.

But so are the calm, easy, cheerful days.

David reminds us here that He sees us in our times of affliction and heart ache. But he also says he rejoices because the Lord sees us there and *then* sets us not only away from the hands of our enemies, but into a spacious place. Room. Room to breathe. Spacious. More than enough. Abundance.

Can you rejoice in the fact that because of His love He sees your affliction and knows the anguish of your soul and promises to deliver you from your enemies and set you in a spacious place?

Here's some truth - even if you can't rejoice yet, take that to Him. He will help you learn to rejoice before, during, and after the season has come and gone. Praying you trust your tender heart to Him.

DAY 32

"You are my hiding place; You will protect me from trouble and surround me with songs of deliverance." Psalm 32:7

Sometimes hiding has a negative connotation. Hiding is sometimes linked to weakness and fear, lack of confrontation and action. However, a hiding place is wise. It's a place to go refocus, catch your breath, a safe spot.

I remember fearing hide and go seek as a little girl. I would hide and then just imagine it being something more serious than a game. I would imagine being found and caught and shame and fear would creep in. As an adult this looks like fearing rest because eventually the 'bad' will find you.

What a beautiful reminder that God is our hiding place. No reason to fear or feel shame. He hides us to help us refocus on His truth. We can hide in Him to renew our spirits. He can be our safe spot. And while there He surrounds us with songs of deliverance. What an incredibly beautiful picture.

What words of deliverance do you think He might be singing to you today?

Praying you allow yourself to hide in His presence today and listen closely for His song to you.

DAY 33

"But the plans of the Lord stand firm forever, the purposes of His heart through all generations." Psalm 33:11

What are the plans of the Lord? He tells us that our thoughts and ways are not His so we can't know His mind completely. But I think it's easy to say that His plans are for continual relationships with His children. His purpose is to share His love and glory with all of us through all generations. That means Baby Boomers, Gen X and Millennials, too.

His plans and purposes will stand firm forever. Because of that, there is *nothing* you could do or not do that would ever keep His plans of loving you and knowing you from happening. He's not gonna change His mind, y'all. He is in constant pursuit of you, *no matter* what you do. (Rom. 8:38)

We make it so complicated, and it really is so simple. He just wants an ongoing authentic relationship with all of us. That's been His plan from the very beginning.

Is there an event or area of your life that is keeping you from Him completely?

Praying we all understand this at a deeper level. That we see through the fallenness of this world and its lies and see more clearly His plans and purposes. His plans to be *with* us, love us, help us and share Himself with us throughout this life no matter what.

DAY 34

"The Lord is close to the broken hearted and saves those who are crushed in spirit." Psalm 34:18

At some point in our lives, we all utter a desperate plea to Him, when we feel our hearts start to crack, when our spirits begin to weaken. "Prevent this! Come quickly! Fix it before it crumbles." There are many times these prayers are answered.

There are many times they are not.

Sometimes hearts break with no warning. The trauma happens almost instantaneously and crushes spirits immediately. Other times we have warnings. We fall to our knees and beg and plead or we pick up our work gloves and get started mending the cracks before they break. And no matter what prayer we pray, no matter how much work we do, it all comes crashing down and we are faced with a new reality that is unbearable.

I do not know why all hearts are not prevented from breaking. I can't answer why all spirits are not crush resistant. I do know for a fact, that when they break…He is there. He is there for you to cry on, yell at, doubt, question, punch, ignore. He is close enough to see the tension in your face, hear the grit of your teeth, and see the tears you try to hide. He does not judge. He does not scold. He does not come telling you how you could have done something to prevent the heartache. He just comes close and does not leave. He stays near.

Can you take a moment in your heart break and imagine Him close to you? Can you find the courage to be fully present and show your deepest thoughts and feelings to Him?

Praying you feel His closeness to any break you may be having. Praying you find the courage to fully show up and when you do, fully feel His presence, comfort, and love surrounding you.

DAY 35

"Lord, You have seen this; do not be silent. Do not be far from me, Lord." Psalm 35:22

When we see others or when we ourselves are in situations of injustice, when consequences of actions do not line up with the accurate motives, we reel and desire immediate revenge. It is an incredibly hard situation to find a loved one being treated unfairly. False accusations, unclear motives, blatant lies. We, like David, beg and plead for restoration, a clearing of a name, justice to be served.

Notice that David asks Him to say something. David has spoken up, tried to defend, prove and plead many times over. However, He learns that only God's words could restore. Only the Creator's voice could set things right.

Rita Springer's song, "Defender" seems to go hand in hand with Psalm 35. He is our Defender. Take heart. You may not see it now, but His way of restoring is so much better than ours.

He sees you. He sees the circumstance. He cares.

Have you asked for His voice in the situation? Have you allowed yourself to quiet and still so you can hear His voice? Can you trust in His *words* and in His *silence?*

Praying if you find yourself helplessly trying to defend yourself or a loved one, you remember who is with you and allow Him to do the defending.

DAY 36

"How priceless is Your unfailing love, O God! People take refuge in the shadow of Your wings. They feast on the abundance of Your house; You give them drink from Your river of delights."
Psalm 36:7-8

When we take refuge under His wing, we find more than we were looking for. We go asking just to be spared from one atrocity. We find a river of delight. We go looking merely to be a slave as the prodigal son hoped when he returned home, and we find a feast of abundance.

Our relationship with Him is unlike any other. All He wants from us is our hearts. Our trust. How often we go begging for scraps and are surprised to find He has an entire banquet prepared for us.

How often do we treat Him as if there is a limited supply? We go to Him unsure of His response to us. Wondering how many times the prodigal can return back home? He even instructs us - 70 times seven. (Matt. 18:21-22) His mercy is abundant. Take in this truth. He doesn't run out. Not of forgiveness, not of joy, not of love, understanding, patience, or desire to be with you.

What area are you only asking from some refuge and would be surprised to know He has a feast of abundance waiting? Where are you fearful to turn to Him not realizing there is a river of delight being offered to you?

Praying we all dare to go boldly before Him as His child. Praying we all get a bigger glimpse of His unfailing love.

Day 37

"Trust in the Lord and do good; dwell in the land and enjoy safe pasture." Psalm 37:3

Our culture seems to always be looking ahead or looking behind. Trying to prepare for the future or prevent the past. Psalm 37 speaks of resting in the present.

He tells us to trust, to dwell, to enjoy. Trust in Him. Dwell in the land. Enjoy safe pasture.

To dwell means to live in. Are you living? Or are you just surviving, preparing, preventing? Are you allowing yourself to be fully present in the moment you're in or are you yearning for the past or worried about the future?

Are you 'in the moment' grasping it because someone has told you to soak in every moment because it will flee quickly? I have read so many well-intentioned articles, been told by good hearted people to not blink because time with my kids, this age, etc. will soon be gone. I don't know about you but that puts even more pressure on me. I think the biggest regret is not words we said or didn't say but allowing fear to steal the gift of the present moment.

Enjoy safe pasture. Trust that with Him even in the valley of the shadows, you are still in safe pasture.

Praying we can learn to dwell. To trust and be and maybe even enjoy a little.

DAY 38

"All my longings lie open before You, Lord; my sighing is not hidden from You." Psalm 38:9

Have you ever had one of those days where you just felt heavy and you knew you needed to 'snap out of it,' but you just couldn't? Maybe you've run out of words to pray? Maybe you feel like a burden on your loved ones and on Him with all these longings that are just ever constant. Chest heavy, energy gone, smile hiding. Maybe not even able to pinpoint what has your heart stirring, but it is the farthest thing from peace.

Read this verse over and over to yourself and take comfort knowing that every single one of those longings is open before Him. They don't annoy Him. He doesn't roll His eyes and walk away. Those sighs that never fully allow a deep enough exhale, He hears them. He understands them. **You are not a burden.** Others may not understand your situation. You may not even understand your situation completely. And that's ok. He does. And He's not demanding you figure it all out right this second. If He can sleep through the middle of a raging storm at sea, your sighs are not bothering Him either. And in His timing those sighs will ease just as those waves.

How does it affect you to know that your longings and sighing are not hidden from Him?

Praying peace in the middle of the sighing today. Praying for His strength to help you hold questions while you wait for answers and relief.

DAY 39

"But now, Lord, what do I look for? My hope is in You."
Psalm 39:7

Psalm 39 speaks of David mourning the fleeting nature of this life. We look back and are just a breath. The span of our time is here over and done quicker than can be imagined.

Isn't that how it seems? As soon as we come to appreciate one season, it's changing. We anticipate and long for the next thing. We blink and it's gone. It is easy to see how despairing that perspective can become. To realize one day all we've worked and longed for on this earth will be gone and possibly forgotten.

But.

When we choose to hope in Him, to give Him each step, season, and event then nothing comes back void. When we place ourselves, our desires, our dreams, goals into His plan, His upper story then we become woven into a much bigger and eternal picture. We have confidence that nothing we have done in His name, hand in hand with The Creator will truly be in vain.

Are you in a season of despair? Do you feel your work is unseen or in vain? Put your hope in Him and know when He becomes involved (in mundane or in grand plans) He breathes eternal life on to it, guaranteeing long lasting fruit.

Praying He allows you to see some of the fruit of your life today.

DAY 40

"I do not hide Your righteousness in my heart; I speak of Your love and Your faithfulness from the great assembly." Psalm 40:10

We were made to be relational. On the same team. This whole God thing is hard. There are days of doubt and days of clarity. There are days of anger and days of peace. He knows that. And from the beginning of creation, He knew we couldn't do it all alone. From Eve, to Jesus, to Holy Spirit and the creation of the Church, He knew we would need people to hold up our arms when we get tired, people to remind us of the light when we remain in darkness.

This is why we cannot keep our stories hidden. The enemy would like you to believe you are too much or not enough. That you should keep silent due to shame and fear. It's a lie. Don't worry about what others may think. The story of faithfulness and love, redemption and hope He is writing on your heart is one someone else needs to hear. Tell it. Tell your story. You don't have to write a book, tour arenas, or speak on a stage. It could be one text message, one encouraging conversation. When you feel the truly awesome hand of God move in your life let others know. When you find yourself on the other side of the tunnel, relieved to see the sun, shout back to those who may still be in the darkness. Even if it just gives one person motivation to keep going, isn't that worth it? Don't keep silent. Speak of His love and faithfulness. We are all in this together.

Do you feel His prompting to share something?

Praying you feel Him as you take one brave step in courage to share.

DAY 41

"Blessed are those who have regard for the weak; the Lord delivers them in times of trouble." Psalm 41:1

Have regard - to think of, to consider

I love the saying 'hurt people hurt people.' We are all hurt people. We are all weak people, too.

What would it look like if we all gave regard to the hidden weaknesses in all of us? Not making excuses for behaviors, but just a regard, consideration.

I've heard many people state they wish they could wear a sign that explains what they are really dealing with. That way people would truly understand their reactions to things. A mom in a grocery store letting her kid act wild - inside she's weak from sleep deprivation and relentless mom guilt. A friend snaps at you - inside they are fighting immense perfectionism. You find out a coworker has been saying hurtful things about you - inside they are struggling with self-esteem and shame issues.

Regarding one another's weaknesses doesn't excuse disrespectful behavior or hurtful actions. However, if we can see beyond ourselves and realize we are all acting and reacting out of places touched by this fallen world then maybe we could all offer a little more grace to one another. Maybe we could find bravery and show up honestly. Regard our weakness and the weaknesses of others. Isn't that what He does daily? He knows we are weak. He came to earth to understand that, literally put Himself in our shoes.

What situation in your life would benefit from considering the weaknesses of others that are involved?

Praying for clarity for all of us. Praying we can come to the table recognizing the weaknesses in all of us and with His power help each other to take those weaknesses to Him.

DAY 42

"My soul is downcast within me; therefore I will remember You." Psalm 42:6

Because my soul is down, I will remember You. Jesus tells us in this world we will have trouble. Our souls will be downcast. But! To take heart because He has overcome this world. (John 16:33)

His thoughts are not our thoughts. His ways are not our ways. If we focus only on the present situation that has us down, we miss out on His ways and thoughts. If we plead for our souls to look up, to refocus on Him then He can show us the glimmers of truth about Himself and the situation. He can remind us of all the many ways He has rescued, aided, loved, brought beauty to, been faithful.

His plan for us is abundant life. Joy. Freedom. With Him. When things around us point to the opposite, may we remember Him, His character and faithfulness.

Do you have some flag posts in your life of times where you can look back and say, "There. There is where He came through and I know He'll do it again. I am not alone."

Praying in hard times we can make the choice to remember Him, to remember His promises and faithfulness.

DAY 43

"Send me Your light and Your faithful care, let them lead me; let them bring me to Your holy mountain to the place where you dwell. Then I will go to the altar of God." Psalm 43:3-4

So many times, we think that we have to go to the altar of God before we can be in the place where He dwells. David shows us it's the opposite.

Send me Your light and care. Bring me to where you are. *Then* I will go to the altar.

False teachings tell us we must sacrifice first in order to receive Him. We must look a certain way or say a specific phrase. It's not true. Jesus sacrificed before we were born. We go to the altar in *response* to His care, not in order to get it. The payment has been paid. You don't and can't earn His presence. It's there right now with you.

Where are you striving to find Him today? Can you trust that His faithful care is there and will guide you to His presence?

Praying we all are led more and more by His light and care and not by our own sacrifices to find His good graces. His grace and care are here in abundance.

DAY 44

"It was not by their sword that they won the land, nor did their arm bring them victory; it was Your right hand, Your arm, and the light of Your face, for You loved them." Psalm 44:3

He does not promise us absence of war, a life without doubts, days untouched by this fallen world. We are all daily affected by one massive domino effect since Eden. None of us will get through untouched.

We have heard God's promise of restoration and peace, joy and great love. But when days get hard and we begin to believe the habitual lies - victory rests on our shoulders, love is only given to those who deserve it, peace will only happen when the chaos calms - we are actually continuing the battle. It is when we realize that victory does not come from the works of our hands, our defenses - it has *already come* from His hand (work), His arm (protection), and the light of His face (joy) because of His great love.

So, if you are tired of fighting, put down your sword, be still and allow Him to show you what He's already done. There is no need to strive here. Rest in Him.

What sword do you need to put down?

Praying you sense His right arm of victory and the light of His face today.

DAY 45

"Led in with joy and gladness, they enter the palace of the king." Psalm 45:15

Psalm 45 is a wedding song. It describes a beautiful one. The groom is painted as a majestic King, the bride glorious and beautiful. She approaches the king with *joy* and *gladness.*

The bride is the church. The church is you. God sees you as glorious. Glorious. Not a burden, not a selfless act to take on, but a waited for bride. He is excited to see you coming to Him!

I firmly believe in the spirit of hoping for humility, many of us have turned to self-deprecation. We think if we state something positive about ourselves then it is bragging. Hear me. It is not. You are beautiful, more than enough, whole, glorious in His eyes. Period. It's not pity that makes Him love you. He just loves you. He can't not love you. You are His bride. He. Chose. You. Walk in the joy of that knowledge.

What is something He has placed in you that makes Him smile?

I pray today you open the door and walk toward Him with joy and gladness as His long-awaited love.

DAY 46

"Be still and know that I am God." Psalm 46:10

"Therefore, we will not fear, though the earth give way and the mountains fall into the heart of the sea." (vs. 2) I've never seen a real mountain fall into the sea or felt the earth truly give way. And though I may not have been an eyewitness to the foundation of the earth shaking, my personal foundation has definitely crumbled. Everything I once thought solid and secure, beliefs and relationships that were part of my core, my identity - gone. Some in a quick moment, some shaking slowly, quietly at first, threatening my stability mentally, emotionally, physically and spiritually. During these moments I have hidden and ignored. Often, I raced, scurried to do all I could to prevent any further foundation desolation. Patch any cracks before they left me torn wide open. Desperately try to rebuild things the way they used to be.

While I appeared strong, brave, noble maybe, I was actually preventing the very thing I was pursuing - peace, wholeness, restoration. Maybe if we want the chaos to go away, it must first begin within. Just be still.

Be still.

Be.

Not do.

Let the "I AM" do what He does. Hear Him as He reminds you, "I AM the peace you seek. I AM the strength you need. I AM the eyes to see through the dust clouds of destruction."

Are you striving and hustling for peace, belonging, forgiveness?

Praying today you can allow yourself to still and remember who He is and what He says about you. You are seen. You are forgiven. You are loved. You are His. Though your mountains may shake, and your seas may roar, "He is within you. You will not fall." (vs. 5)

DAY 47

"God has ascended amid shouts of joy." Psalm 47:5

Have you ever experienced a moment and it take over you? In that moment have you embraced that, or have you felt conscious of it, afraid that maybe you are 'overreacting?'

In chapter 47 we are urged to sing praises, shout to God, sound the trumpets. All those things take up a lot of space. They make a disturbance in the air. They are LOUD. But they are important. And because we are on the resurrection side of Christ, we know that the ascension of God means more than the ark going up to the Temple. Our High Priest has ascended to His throne because it is finished!

He ascended amid *shouts* of JOY. Be loud. Be bold. Be JOYFUL. When we fully understand that It. Is. Finished and He has won, then joyful shouts make so much sense.

Where do you need to proclaim shouts of joy towards a situation that does not yet seem joyful?

Praying you are bold in proclaiming joy even if you feel it is in vain. He rises among shouts of joy *because He's already won.* That's definitely cause to celebrate!

DAY 48

"God is in her citadels. He has shown Himself to be her fortress." Psalm 48:3

Citadel - strong shelter/place of safety

Fortress - person not susceptible to outside influence or disturbance

God is in our place of safety. He is our place of safety. We look over our walls and see the enemies approaching - not with sharp weapons riding horses threatening our security or with bows taut aiming arrows straight for us. We see the enemy approach with final notice bills in the mailbox, an unexpected diagnosis, an unmet expectation. The list could go on. The enemy knows the weak spots around the walls of your personal castle.

But God is in our citadels. He is in our safe shelter. He has shown Himself to be our fortress. He does not give in to outside influence or disturbance. It doesn't faze Him. The diagnosis, the account with a much lower number than we would like, the voice in your head that is so loud you would swear it has to be truth. None of this scare or surprise Him. He can handle it. He makes us secure forever. (vs. 8)

Are you feeling your foundation crack? Do you feel a little insecure? Remember who is in your citadel. Remember who has proven Himself to be your fortress again and again and again and *will continue to be forever.*

I pray today you look at those enemies coming to taunt you and sing His praises over them. Trust and remember He has you and He has that which is coming to threaten your security.

DAY 49

"But God will redeem me from the realm of the dead; He will surely take me to Himself." Psalm 49:15

This may be one of the most beautiful verses in all of scripture. We have all been in the realm of the dead. Joyless, in a rut, dark. Seasons where it seems you are just getting by, not sure what you are living for, or if you are truly even "living."

What a bold, hopeful statement. Once the psalmist recognizes he is, in fact, in the realm of the dead, he also knows God will take him to where He is. A place far from death. A place brimming with continuous new creation, life, light, hope, joy.

I do not know exactly what your 'realm of dead' may look like. But if there is any part of you, any area of your life that feels it is needing some life - your job, a relationship, a womb...know that He redeems and He comes to you and brings you back to His realm of life.

Note the wordage there, "*He* will surely *take me* to Himself." It's not on your shoulders. You don't work for it; you don't earn it. You just ask for it. He comes to you!

Is there a specific area in your life that just feels dead? Have you acknowledged it to yourself? Once you recognize it and own it, you are then free to ask Him to take you from it. He will bring that area to Himself. In His presence is peace, hope, joy, and life.

Praying you feel Him gently bring you to His presence today.

DAY 50

"I know every bird in the mountains, and the insects in the fields are mine." Psalm 50:11

He knows every bird. Have you ever stopped and just imagined how many birds there must be flying above us or sitting on electric poles? Now imagine how many are in the hidden forests on the mountains. He knows them. He knows their habits. He knows their songs. He knows where they nest.

The insects in the field. How many small and seemingly insignificant little creatures do we walk over without a second thought? The ants, the caterpillars, the spiders and all the other creepy crawlers. He claims them, y'all. And we wonder if He cares about us?

The little thing that has been 'bugging' you, of course He cares about it! Ever feel like you are so deep in a forest that no one knows or cares about your habits, songs, dreams and desires? Think again! There are birds out there no human has ever seen and yet He knows them. There are insects that will be born and will live their whole lives unseen by any 'important' people. He claims them as His own. You are not alone. You are not insignificant. You are known and you are claimed.

May you be reminded by the pigeon, black bird, robin and red bird that you are known deeply. May the next insect that crosses your path remind you that you are claimed by the Mighty Creator of animals, insects, you, and Love.

DAY 51

"Renew a steadfast spirit within me." Psalm 51:10

The only things certain in this world are change and Jesus. Our hearts are influenced by all the shifting and changing around us. We are all alive, therefore we are all growing...changing. It is easy in uncertain times, shifting seasons, to forget our foundation. We question identities, we wrestle with our beliefs. It can be scary and unsettling. These changes sway us, give us different viewpoints. "What if His promises aren't true?"
But Jesus. He is our steadfast spirit. Steadfast, loyal, reliable, true.

It is ok to doubt. He wants us to wrestle with it. It shows we are seeking to grasp Truth. He understands the complexities of this faith. When our faith seems not so steadfast, I believe we should *press on* into the fight. If we had all the answers, it wouldn't be faith.

David asks God for a renewed spirit. A spirit that is loyal, devoted, that looks at the big questions and says, "I may not understand, but I'm not giving up. I may not have all the answers, but that's ok."

I've spent many years, many seasons doubting. You are not alone in that. Just don't let your spirit stop searching. Ask Him (even if you doubt Him) for a steadfast spirit to not give up, to keep seeking for peace, answers, and presence.

Is there something particular you have been questioning, struggling with? Know you can take it to Him no matter how big or small.

Ask Him to renew a steadfast spirit within you to give you perseverance for this race. This race you may not even believe you are running. The finish line out of sight, maybe even imagined. We all need encouragement when we doubt along the way. He will renew you. Ask Him.

DAY 52

"But I am like an olive tree flourishing in the house of God;
I trust in God's unfailing love for ever and ever." Psalm 52:8

Olive trees typically flourish in desert like areas. A beautiful picture of strength and resilience. Flourishing in the midst of arid and barren lands. This is a jarring juxtaposition. Flourishing. Barren. It is pretty easy to see what David could have been talking about. If we trust in the unfailing love in the dry and barren land, then we will flourish. We can fight the good fight and prove we can overcome hard times.

It struck me that David was sure to say he was like an olive tree that flourished in the house of God, not in the desert. Why would he choose to paint that particular picture?

I believe some of us have fought to flourish in the desert for so long that we forget there is more landscape in which to grow. Yes, we can bloom there, despite all odds, fighting all the elements. But we can also flourish in His abundance. We can flourish while we rest at home. Some of us have been in the desert so long that when we become uprooted and planted in His house, we fear the change of environment. We are so accustomed to challenging circumstances that we either don't trust the abundance and its stability or we fear we will not be able to prove ourselves. It would be too 'easy' to blossom here. I will be overlooked. Some of us (myself included) try to change the climate to a more difficult one because that's where we believe blooming has to happen.

When we trust in His unfailing love, we do what we were made to do. No matter the environment. No matter the season of life you are in.

Are you afraid to allow yourself to be planted in His house because you think your worth comes from flourishing in a hostile environment?

I am praying we all will focus on His unfailing love regardless of our situation. He wants you to grow, bloom, flourish in the hard times and in the easier ones. Look to Him. This is not a test. That's not who He is. Focus on Him and flourishing will be inevitable.

DAY 53

"But there they are, overwhelmed with dread where there was nothing to dread. God scattered the bones of those who attacked you." Psalm 53:5

This verse contains so much. It is easy to interpret it from the reader's point of view. And how true, so many times we ourselves are downtrodden with dread and soon realize there was nothing to dread in the first place. What a great feeling, the exhale of all exhales. And while it is true, we waste so much time dreading and fearing I don't believe we are the subject of this verse.

David is writing about the enemies encamped around the Israelites. Verse four says they are devouring His people as though eating bread. But suddenly fear and dread overwhelmed them (the enemy.) For no apparent reason, the enemies began to lose their confidence.

I can't imagine the change in the atmosphere. One minute the Israelites are fearing for their lives and the next the enemies are the ones suddenly so afraid. They stop terrorizing the Israelites. And God took care of the rest.

God scattered enemy bones away from His people. *He didn't tell His people to fight harder.* He didn't pat the enemies on the head and tell them to please go away. He saw His beloved being devoured and put an end to it. He took what they were trying to give to the Israelites - fear, dread, death, and gave it right back to the ones it came from. And the good news for us? He's done that very thing to the main source of all our confusion, dread, and fear. Because of Jesus, our enemy's bones are scattered!

Are you feeling overwhelmed with dread, fear, worry? Maybe He's not asking you to fight harder. Maybe He's about to spin all that right on back to the enemy where it came from.

Praying you remember the bones of those who attacked you are scattered! They do not have power over you! Live from that truth. May that be what overwhelms you.

DAY 54

"Surely God is my help; the Lord is the One who sustains me." Psalm 54:4

Why is it that when we get into a difficult situation, we tend to scurry away to fix it by ourselves? Our God is not one who tells us to get it all together before we come to Him. He is not surprised by our weaknesses. Our fears do not scare Him. Our major mishaps do not surprise Him.

David wrote this psalm after a betrayal resulting in more turmoil. Turmoil along the path to the throne he was told was his. God anointed him as king and then sat another man on the throne. Throughout the years David and Saul had many a hard time. None of this was news to God. None of this swayed David. He remembered his place. He reminded himself where his help came from. *The one that anointed him would be the one that would sustain him when all looked far from the promise.*

Are you looking around wondering when His call for you will finally take place? Do you wonder if you heard Him wrong all those years ago?

If you feel betrayed by a circumstance or another person, remember that God is your help. He will sustain you all the way. Praying you know this deeply today.

DAY 55

"As for me, I call to God, and the Lord saves me. Evening, morning and noon I cry out in distress, and He hears my voice. He rescues me unharmed from the battle waged against me." Psalm 55:16-18

God's patience level is unlike any we can understand. There is no amount of pleading to Him that will cause Him to turn away. You are not a bother to Him. He does not get angry at you for continuing to bring Him a concern.

Some think if we had enough faith, we wouldn't think about the issues anymore. I can understand that point, but we are human. Know that if you have a tendency to worry, He wants you to bring your cares to Him. "Cast all your anxiety on Him because He cares for you." 1 Peter 5:7

David reminds us no matter what time of day or how many times a day, He hears our voice when we call out to Him. And not only that, but He also rescues us unharmed from the battle raging against us.

The key is not to have enough strength, stamina, faith, etc. to fight it out on our own. It's not about downplaying the effects an issue has on us because we don't want to be weak. It's all about taking those concerns and telling Him about them. That's where we grow. That's where problems are solved. That's where the battle is fought.

Are there concerns, worries, fears you are dealing with on your own, not talking to Him about them because you don't want to be a bother or appear not strong enough? Are you believing the lie that He doesn't have enough time or care about your details?

My prayer for you right now is that you know and trust He cares about the desires of your heart. (Psalm 37:4) Do not try to do it all on your own. Talk to Him, yell at Him, cry to Him evening, morning and noon. He will rescue you. Give Him the chance.

DAY 56

"When I am afraid, I put my trust in You." Psalm 56:3

There are countless times in scripture when He tells us not to be afraid. I love that David is honest here. He doesn't try to force his fear away. He doesn't deny it. He brings it to God.

This psalm was written after he had been captured. Of course, he was afraid! Even the melody he used was significant. It is written to the tune of "A Dove on Distant Oaks." Doves represent peace and Holy Spirit. He did not feel peace. He did not feel Him close. But. He still took his fear to Him and claimed through his fear he trusted Him.

If you are afraid, tell Him. Ask Him for help in trusting Him in the middle of an uncertain, scary time.

Where is fear gripping you?

Praying you can release it and trust in Him today.

DAY 57

"I will take refuge in the shadow of Your wings until the disaster has passed." Psalm 57:1b

David fled from danger into a cave and there he wrote these beautiful words. While hiding and afraid he recognized the darkness was actually God's comfort and protection. He took refuge in the shadow of His wings and continued to declare His glory and greatness there despite what his surroundings looked like.

There are times we are called to face it all head on and fight with the strength He gives. But I believe more often than not, He calls us into caves, shadow comforts under His wings while we trust and rest, regaining strength to sing out and remind ourselves of His glory and faithfulness.

I believe our most transformative and mighty moments come not from traditional battle, but from singing out His praises *during* the war. To fight against every logical thought and sing ourselves back to the truths He has proven all along. Even when it looks bleak and vastly different from His promise.

There is power in praise. There is refuge in the hidden caves. There is hope in the dark shadow of His wings.

David specifically mentions wings, not just one wing. The only way to be in the shadow of both wings is for them to be wrapped around you. The darkness does not mean you are alone. Quite the opposite.

David's story did not end there in the cave. The anointing remained true, and he eventually took his promised seat.

Do you find yourself somewhere that looks far from His promise?

I pray you know the story isn't over. "He sends from heaven and saves [you], God sends forth His love and His *faithfulness*." (vs. 3)

DAY 58

"Let them vanish like water that flows away; when they draw the bow, let their arrows fall short." Psalm 58:7

Enemies are a part of life. They do not look today like they looked when the psalms were written. Few of us flee into literal caves to avoid flying arrows or put on physical armor to fight giants for rights to property and identity. However, we war for those things even today.

Our enemies are not as easily seen. The disguises have advanced. We see them in many advertisements when we doubt our security because ads tell us we should have the next greatest thing. We hear them in our head. The lies that tell us we are no longer good enough because of status, weight, bank accounts, job titles, relationships, etc. The enemy of comparison shoots many arrows.

Our greatest enemy comes to steal, kill and destroy. (John 10:10) Steal peace, kill joy, destroy love. **Anything that does this to you is an enemy.** Our Creator, Father, King does not wish destruction for us. He comes to bring ABUNDANT life.

Where in your life do you feel your peace has been stolen, your joy killed, your love (for Him, others, and yourself) destroyed?

My prayer for today is this verse. May those enemies vanish like water that flows away. When they draw their bow, may their arrows fall short. May you be reminded today of what He says about you and your life. May you begin to feel the abundance of it. You are chosen. You are enough. You are competent. You are loved. Fight your war with these truths as the deceitful water flows away and the enemy arrows fall short.

DAY 59

"You are my strength, I watch for You; You God are my fortress, my God in whom I can rely." Psalm 59:9-10

The last three psalms have all been written to the same tune, "Do Not Destroy," and are all penned in the middle of a threat. David wrote Psalm 59 when Saul had sent men to stalk his house in order to kill him.

When seized by a nation (Ps. 56), hiding in a cave (Ps. 57), surrounded by stalkers (Ps. 59) he called out for protection and justice. He claimed God as his strength and fortress.

David does not write this verse after the enemy is gone. He writes it *while* they are encamped around him. This is at least the third time he has been in a life-threatening situation and yet, he still says that he can rely on God.

What perspective. It would be easy to look at the situation - far from the promise, and doubt Him, blame Him, lose all faith in Him. My mind would easily go to, "I asked You for help and here we are again in another trauma." But David, known for seeing God's heart, knows that his only way out of this, His only hope is God.

"I watch for You," (vs. 9). David doesn't see Him yet, but still claims Him as his fortress. He can rely on Him because He has proven Himself faithful in the trials he's already come through.

Are you feeling surrounded by enemies once again?

My prayer for you is to remember you can rely on Him. May you be reminded of how He has already been a fortress for you and how He will continue to be.

DAY 60

"Give us aid against the enemy, for human help is worthless." Psalm 60:11

It seems an easy concept to grasp, but in reality, it can be such a struggle. Be it pride or fear, when times get tough it's easy to turn to other things for help instead of God. We don't want to bother Him. We want to prove we are just fine on our own. We don't want to admit that we really need help.

Whatever the reason, human help without God in it is eventually worthless. Money runs out. Beauty fades. Health succumbs to mortality. Knowledge is ever evolving. Relationships change. But when we line those things up with Him and seek His voice first "we will gain the victory." (vs. 12)

Is there an area where you are needing victory? Have you tried all you know to try, and nothing seems to be working?

Take it to Him. He already sees it. He *wants* to help you. He's not mad. There's no shame. He's not disappointed. He's already won the victory *for* you. Ask Him to show you the way to it.

DAY 61

"I long to dwell in Your tent forever and take refuge in the shelter of Your wings." Psalm 61:4

Note that David does not seek to dwell in the law forever, but in the tent. It could easily be assumed he was referring to the tent that held the Ark of the Covenant - the very presence of God.

When times got hard David longs for His presence. It wasn't the laws he sought. It wasn't the presence of others. It wasn't his homeland. It was God's presence. And in God's presence, David found shelter under His wings.

He knew no matter what the situation was, He could go to Him and find comfort. The presence of God would wrap Him up in comfort and protection.

We are so blessed we do not have to find a tent, a tabernacle, an Ark of the Covenant in order to find His presence. It is always with you.

Could your longing be met in His presence?

I pray you may feel and know that presence and in it you will find His comfort and refuge.

DAY 62

"Trust in Him at all times, you people; pour out your hearts to Him for God is our refuge." Psalm 62:8

Pour out your hearts. Like Mary who broke her vessel over His feet, nothing is wasted. You will never be too much. You are always enough.

So often we believe we must fix our thoughts and feelings before we take them to Him, scared of what He might think or say. He knows them already! He understands why you think and feel the way you do. He created you and He has firsthand experience of being a human Himself. Nothing you think or feel will surprise Him or disappoint Him.

Know that He is always wanting to engage with you. He is where your peace and wisdom are found. He is your safe place. Do not let society, old assumptions and lies stand in the way of fellowshipping with Him. Trust Him as you pour out your precious heart. He is our refuge.

What are you holding back from Him afraid of how He would receive it?

Praying today you let it all go.

DAY 63

"Because You are my help I sing in the shadow of Your wings." Psalm 63:7

Here we find David in a desert. He opens this psalm earnestly seeking God as he does water in a dry and parched land. (vs. 1) He tells himself he will be satisfied as with the richest of foods. (vs. 5) David is taking a cue from the creator and *calling truth out of darkness.*

At creation God saw truth in the vast expanse. Though there was nothing, He called out all that we now know. This is an *ongoing* event. He is continuously creating and even while you are surrounded by darkness, He still creates light. He reminds us to call out truth in the midst of the lies. Because He is our help we can sing in the dark because we know we are under His wings of protection and comfort.

No matter your current view, regardless of what your situation looks like right now cling to the Creator. Remember that He can take the darkest of dark and create LIFE. You will not be in the desert forever. While you wait, sing. While you hunger remember the richest of foods He has provided and be satisfied knowing that He is your help.

What can you sing to Him today? How has He been your help?

Praying you clearly see His help along the way.

DAY 64

"They will proclaim the works of God and ponder what He has done." Psalm 64:9

Proclaim - admit it. Announce it. Tell it.

Ponder - think about. Reflect on. Consider

Ponder. Not understand. Not agree with. Not trust with no doubts. Just simply ponder.

I think a lot of times we get caught in the idea that in order to proclaim we must fully understand. We don't want to look naive, silly, unknowledgeable. It is easy to not proclaim to ourselves and others when we feel Him move in our lives. If there is a chance to 'explain it away' then we chalk it up to coincidence or us being 'crazy.'

But here we see we can first proclaim and then ponder. Admit He's involved and then think about how. Consider such an act. And be ok with knowing you may not fully understand the inner workings of His movement. He doesn't expect us to do so. If He did, we wouldn't need any faith. We wouldn't have to trust Him.

What experience have you had that you could proclaim His movement, but haven't? Have you pondered on it? Does not fully understanding keep you from proclaiming?

I pray you take a step toward trusting even without fully understanding. Move towards proclaiming His mighty works and take comfort that He wants you to ponder on what He has done.

DAY 65

"The whole earth is filled with awe at Your wonders, where morning dawns, where evening fades, You call forth songs of joy."
Psalm 65:8

In new, fresh, hopeful beginnings and each darkening, unsure ending He still calls forth songs of joy. While it may be easiest to sing joyful songs and have a hopeful heart during the dawns of this life, He still provides reasons to sing even in the unsure nightfall.

There are lightning bugs, crickets, stars and moonlight that bring wonder, peace and even joy as unsteadiness sets in during the night. Take heart knowing that at the dawn of creation He thought to bring these reminders of His presence and hope during the nightfall to remind you that you aren't alone even in your unsure season. Remember that with each dusk there is a dawn, and neither will last forever. Though the circumstances change, He doesn't. You find Him in different ways.

Where once you felt His presence like the full blazing noon day sun, now you may see Him in quick glimpses scattered around like mysterious lightning bugs. He remains all the same.

He is constantly calling out to you through your days and seasons to remind you of His love, power, glory, and wonder.

It is not your job to keep night from coming. It is inevitable. But so is His comfort and presence from dawn to dusk.

Praying you see Him in sunlight and lightning bugs today.

DAY 66

"We went through fire and water, but You brought us to a place abundance." Psalm 66:12

So often I find myself trying to prevent the fire and water. However, just like nightfall, it is inevitable. It's not necessarily something I did or did not do. It's not necessarily a punishment. It's just a part of this fallen world.

But it's not permanent. It's not pointless. There is something to learn. He doesn't leave us there. He brings us out. And not just out to a place without fire and flood, but to a place of abundance.

Over and over, we see it's not just that He wants us to be spared of hell. He wants *abundance* for us. Here. Now. Not *just* when we get to Heaven. This abundance begins and ends with Him, communing with Him, laughing with Him, crying with Him, even fighting with Him. Life *with* Him. Emmanuel.

Where do you see abundance in your life?

May you find Him and His abundance with you no matter where you are.

DAY 67

"May God be gracious to us and bless us and make His face shine on us." Psalm 67:1

This simple sentence beautifully shows so much of God's character and His heart.

First, Grace. He has shown the ultimate grace and mercy in Jesus' death and resurrection. He chooses to not give us what we truly deserve.

Then, not only do we not pay for our faults, but He blesses us on top of that! He doesn't want us to just clean up our messy rooms, He wants to fill them backup with good things for us.

Finally, He shows us His face. He forgives and cleans the mess, blesses with good things and then says, "I want to hang out in this room with you!" He wants a relationship with you, not just a robotic obedience to ensure a clean room. He didn't have to do even the first one.

He didn't have to show mercy and grace. He is all righteous, pure, and holy. Yet, He forgave. I feel most of us stop here. Afraid to want, hope, expect anything else. But He's not us. He showers us with abundant blessings and continues. He did all of this to have *relationship* with you. His face shines upon you offering you all that He is.

Have you only thought of Him in one of those areas - grace and mercy, blessings, relationship?

My prayer is that we all begin to see each of those beautiful characteristics of Him and invite Him into what He has so beautifully created for each of us.

DAY 68

"Summon Your power, God; show us Your strength, our God, as you have done before." Psalm 68:28

How often do we take on a problem alone, afraid to let others know, too prideful to ask God for help? There is a false mindset that says, "This problem is too small to take to Him. He's got bigger things to worry about." All the while He's patiently waiting for you to ask Him to summon power and show strength. He is proud of you. He gets to be the one to take care of you and all your worries. He tells us to cast it all on Him yet so often, we carry it on our own. When we do that, we unnecessarily burden ourselves, rob others of seeing Him move, and miss experiencing Him on deeper levels.

He's not a limited God. He's unlimited. He wants you to ask time and time again because He wants to answer each and every time! This is relationship. I believe His power is always around, but our eyes are not always open to it. So, ask. Ask to see it. Ask to see Him move in power and strength. He longs to care for you. He longs to restore you. When Adam and Eve felt shame in the garden (due to their own consequence), He still stooped to make them clothing to hide their shame.

Where might you be hiding, afraid to ask Him for help?

My prayer is that we go boldly before Him and ask Him for His power and strength to come to our rescue again and again. It's who He is. It's what He does,

DAY 69

"You who seek God, may your hearts live!" Psalm 69:32

David begins this chapter calling out in utter despair. He is drowning, engulfed in floods. He is worn out calling for help. His eyes fail trying to see Him. (vs. 1-3)

Yet later he encourages those who still seek Him. May your hearts live!

David has learned a tough truth. *The answer comes in the seeking.* How easy it would be if we just knew automatically - the job we should take, the person we should date, the location to move, the way to ease the pain. However, would quickly knowing the answer allow us to know The Answer as deeply?

God doesn't hide. His presence continuously surrounds us. But because of a fallen world, we sometimes are forced to wait for answers. And in that waiting He takes an unpleasant situation and brings life and goodness out of it. He sometimes teaches us more of His character in the waiting than He does in the answer.

Are worn out from calling for help and feel you are drowning?

I pray you keep seeking, keep praising. It's there. You will find The Answer and your heart will live. (vs. 30-32)

DAY 70

"I am poor and needy; come quickly to me, O God. You are my help and my deliverer." Psalm 70:5

Why does the word needy have such a negative connotation? We live in a society that boasts in complete independence or falls into heavy co-dependence. We are called to live *inter*dependently. Which means, we need each other and more importantly, we need Him. But for some reason we never want to come across as one who has needs. And on the reverse side we all want our loved ones to just tell us what they need! How many times have we said, "I can't read your mind!"

There is NO SHAME for admitting you have needs. None. Being needy for Jesus is not a bad thing. We were never meant to try to live this life without needing Him. And While He actually *can* read our minds, it is still important for us to voice our needs before Him. It helps us to see what we need more clearly and in return better see how He meets the need. It doesn't make you weak. It strengthens your faith and your relationship with your Help and Deliverer.

Can you be a little more vulnerable and share with Him a need you have - big or small? Give Him the chance to help and deliver.

DAY 71

"My tongue will tell of your righteous acts all day long"
Psalm 71:24

Proverbs tells us the power of life and death is in the tongue (18:21). What we say to ourselves and to others is important and powerful.

When our circumstances don't seem to fit what we have been told of God we are faced with a crisis of faith. Do we come into agreement with our circumstances, or do we come into agreement with what He's shown us about Himself?

This does not mean that you push aside what you feel and even what you fear. It is important to acknowledge those. Likewise, it's just as important to speak out loud the truth of who He is *regardless* of what we feel or fear. Speaking it out loud helps our hearts and minds to focus on the truth. It realigns our spirits with His.

Can we speak of His righteousness all day long even when circumstances are frustrating, and hope seems to be gone? If you cannot speak it, find someone who can speak it to you as a reminder.

What are some truths of His righteousness that you can speak today? Maybe your words can encourage someone else who needs reminders.

Praying you are flooded with truths today.

DAY 72

"May the crops flourish…and thrive." Psalm 72:16

Some say that Solomon penned these words from a prayer of blessing from his father, David. It is a psalm full of a king's hopes and requests for his son, the future king.

How easy a concept to embrace - a parent wishing blessing for their child. How much more does God, The Father want to bless us! The psalmist wishes for crops to not just flourish but thrive. Not just one bloom, but an abundance. How many of us only meekly ask for a small bloom when He's ready to give us a thriving abundance? How many of us quit asking as the rain falls, afraid that's a sign of punishment or abandonment when in all actuality it will cause the very bloom and abundance we ask for?

How much longer until we get the clear picture in our head of Him as a loving Father who teaches and gives blessing through the downpour and turns storms into the very thing that helps us thrive?

I challenge you to go boldly before Him to talk, to honor, to request, to listen, to sit in stillness and reflect on what He's given, what He's giving and what He's going to give. Learn more of who He truly is each day. Flourish and thrive with the Creator.

How has He brought flourishing into your life?

Praying your heart leans into the truth that He wants good things for you, His child.

DAY 73

"Whom have I in Heaven but You? And earth has nothing I desire besides You." Psalm 73:25

Bitterness, comparison, envy - it is so easy to look around at others and imagine what it must be like to live their life. We see what they do and see the seemingly lack of consequences and grow angry. In my own life it leads to thoughts similar to verse 13, "Surely in vain I have kept my heart pure." The psalmist continues to lament until verses 16-17, "When I tried to understand all this, it troubled me deeply till I entered the sanctuary of God."

When the psalmist took their eyes off their own surroundings and entered God's sanctuary understanding came. Our focus so easily goes to those around us, wanting to make sure we get our fair share of what we have done. We completely miss the point. When we turn our gaze to Him, we better understand that there is nothing better on earth or in Heaven than Him. In Him we find the creator of all the things we desire. We have the source, not just of material things, but of fullness, peace, love, joy. There is truly nothing greater on this earth than Him.

What steals your focus from Him?

Praying you can release your gaze from a good thing in order to focus on the Creator of all that is Good, Holy, Beautiful and Loving.

DAY 74

"Have regard for Your covenant, because haunts of violence fill the dark places of the land." Psalm 74:20

At times, our surroundings are so dark and bleak, so far from what we've been promised we wonder if God forgot what He said. Even the psalmist encourages God to remember the covenant He made - to bless Abraham and his people.

How comforting to know we do not anger God when we think we have to remind Him of who He is. *The reminding is truly for ourselves.* He has not forgotten the promise He made to you. No matter what your surroundings may look like, no matter what the report or the person said. If He promised you something you can consider it done.

Are you in the middle of a dark place waiting on a fulfilled promise?

His ways are not our ways, and we may not ever understand. Know He has not forgotten you or His promise even if it looks and feels like He has.

DAY 75

"When the earth and all its people quake, it is I who hold its pillars firm." Psalm 75:3

God does not promise constant steadiness, a life without change, stress, or wondering. He does promise that in the middle of quaking He holds the pillars firm.

It is not our job to steady the earth or its people. He holds us firm even amid the shaking. You cannot do it within your own strength. Not for yourself. Not for anyone else.

The psalm continues to basically say, don't boast in your own strength. Listen. He does not expect us to do this whole life thing on our own. When the foundations crack and everything shakes, He's not going to come in from another room surprised or disappointed that everything seems to be in shambles. He's in the room when it happens and He's the one that's keeping it from falling all the way down on our heads.

You are not responsible for holding up your pillars or anyone else's. He's got this.

What pillars are you trying to hold on to instead of letting Him?

Praying for release and rest for you.

DAY 76

"At Your rebuke, God of Jacob, both horse and chariot lie still." Psalm 76:6

No matter if something is God made or human made, it falls under His command. The wind and waves and naturally occurring incidents of this fallen world or our own man made plans and creations are ultimately His.

God is fierce with anything that gets in His way to His people. Be encouraged that all things will lie still under His word. He is to be feared not because He is scary, but because we cannot grasp His power. He uses this power to reconcile with His children. No horse or chariot will stand in His way.

Is there something in your life that needs to take a break and lie still?

Praying you find the ability either by your decision or His to be still today.

DAY 77

"I will remember Your miracles of long ago." Psalm 77:11

It is so easy to get absorbed into the heavy and dark that can surround us. There will be times when God feels far away. We wonder if He's forgotten us. "Did I make all of that up?"

The early portion of this psalm shows the distress of humanity. The writer remembers God...and groans with a faint spirit. He does not remember God and shout for joy or remember God and everything snaps back into place.

Later, while he is still in distress and still seeking God, He remembers what God has already done, what He's already proven about Himself and His faithfulness. The writer's spirit doesn't come across as changed. However, his focus sure does. And when focus goes from the present distress to remembering what God has already done, the text no longer mentions the longing and aching. I'm sure it's still there, but now there is opportunity for hope to be present as well.

Do not diminish the size of your troubles; you have them. They are likely large. But while you are looking at those, remind yourself of what God's already shown you about His character. Remember who He is and what He has done for others and for you.

Is there an area of your life where your focus could shift from troubles to Him?

Praying He reminds you of how He's been faithful and mighty in previous days.

DAY 78

"But He brought His people out like a flock; He led them like sheep through the wilderness." Psalm 78:52

The verses prior to this one retells the exodus of Egypt. It states details and reminders of how God rescued them. I wonder why He didn't have the Egyptians leave so His people could stay? Why did His people have to be brought out like a flock?

I'm sure there are countless studies done for this answer. I'm not 100% sure why they had to leave. I am sure though that He led them. He led them like sheep, gently. They cried out for their enslavement to end. He could have brought equality within the land, but instead, He took them out of the land that held them hostage and guided them to His promised land for them.

If you are in a situation where your throat is raw from crying out for justice and mercy know He hears you. Sometimes He changes the circumstances where we are and sometimes, He takes us to completely new lands.

Do you feel things are completely changing for you? Are you feeling led out to some place new?

May you know He is gently and safely guiding you to His promised land for you.

DAY 79

"May the groans of the prisoners come before You; with Your strong arm preserve those condemned to die." Psalm 79:11

It has always bothered me to read the stories of war and the violent revenge requested throughout a lot of the Old Testament. I don't have scholarly answers, but through my readings over the years, God has shown me these passages can become repeatable if the adversaries mentioned are thought of as the day to day struggles we face. I don't believe that challenges great and small are sent as hoops for us to jump through. I believe the struggles we face, the adversaries, are all a result of the fallen world. And we must remember He fights to free us from those effects. The battle is ultimately won with Jesus, but we are still in the middle of fighting the after effects of the fall.

So, when we read chapters such as this one, we find hope in knowing we are not alone during our bleak seasons. Chapter 79 was written following Nebuchadnezzar's invasion and capture. The psalmist calls out for God to hear the groans of those imprisoned, beckons for His strong arm to save those that are on the brink of death. And just as the psalmist did not know what was ahead, we don't either. However, we know of His faithfulness, His ultimate victory and His omnipresence with us no matter our circumstance.

The psalm ends with "from generation to generation we will proclaim Your praise."

Raise a hallelujah in your bleak season. Cry out for Him to hear your imprisoned groans no one else hears. His strong arm will preserve you.

Is there someone imprisoned by something that you feel led to plead to God for them?

I pray for those who are trapped by lies today. For those that are imprisoned and don't even know it. For those who are imprisoned and don't have the strength to fight it anymore. May His strong arm preserve them.

DAY 80

"Let Your hand rest on the man at Your right hand, the son of man You have raised up for Yourself." Psalm 80:17

'The man at Your right hand' can represent a few things - Israel, a king, a priest. Ultimately, we know it is Jesus.

A hand resting on someone often symbolizes strength, protection and blessing. Other versions read the end of the verse as "the son of man whom You have made strong for Yourself."

Jesus is at the right hand. God's hand is resting on Him offering Him strength, protection and blessings. We know this right-hand man, Jesus, is protected and strong and He sits at His right hand interceding for you. The one God raised up and put His hand of protection, strength and blessing on is sitting next to Him talking to Him about you.

He's been put through all the tests and fully knows and feels what you are going through. When words fail you, He takes that knowledge from His experience here and pleads on your behalf.

You aren't alone. You don't have to fight alone.

How does it feel to know that your name has been uttered in prayer from Jesus? That right now He is on your side and is rooting for you. He is for you.

DAY 81

"I removed the burden from their shoulders; their hands were set free from the basket. In your distress you called, and I rescued you." Psalm 81:6-7

He removes the circumstances of burden that simply fall on us. The ones we have no control over. They just happened. The burden of a loss of a job, a change in a friendship, a diagnosis. These things are literally out of our hands, but we still feel the weight of them all. He takes the burden for us.

He removes the circumstances of burdens we choose to pick up and carry. The heavy baskets filled with expectations. These expectations we carry from one situation to the next. Good expectations, bad expectations. Our assumptions of what "should" happen or what a certain situation 'should' look like. Those little things add up to a basket full of heavy. He removes our hands from them. And reminds us He is here.

He has brought you out of Egypt. You have access to the promised land. He is for you. Recognizing His true presence and true character of wanting to rescue you, lead you, be with you will ease the burden of life and help you forget about the basket of expectations we carry.

He calls us to keep our mind and heart on Him.

How can you take one small step of trust today? What burden do you need Him to rescue from you? Is there a basket you are still carrying?

I pray you feel Him gently take your hands off it.

DAY 82

"Rescue the weak and the needy." Psalm 82:4

Needs are ok. We try to hide them for fear of burdening others, burdening God. Yet, what a privilege it is to help others in their time of need.

Don't deny others or Him the blessing of being there with you in the middle of your darkest night. He cares for you, for all the smallest details. He does not want you to 'fix all the things' before you come to Him. That's backwards.

Be honest. Tell Him what your needs are. Tell Him where you are struggling. If you can't find the words, He knows your spirit. Show it to Him. Let Him rescue you. You don't have to be strong all the time.

Where are you needy and weak?

Praying you give these areas to Him today. Fully admitting your weakness and needs. You are not a burden. Allow Him to rescue you today.

DAY 83

"[to those] who said, 'Let us take possession of the pasturelands of God.' Make them like tumbleweed, my God, like chaff before the wind." Psalm 83:12-13

The pasturelands of God. Some commentaries state this could represent wherever God has dwelt. If we take that to mean within our own souls, then we see the plea of the psalmist. Anyone who goes after what God has placed inside of us, may they tumble and blow away like chaff in the wind.

Do you have a calling you feel He has placed within you? Is there a time when you know you were within His pastureland? There is nothing that can overcome that. Anything that tries to take possession of your place in Him can be rolled away like tumbleweed, like the stone that rolled out of His way. His plan will be fulfilled.

His plan for you. His plan for the kingdom. His plan includes peace, restoration, love and His glory.

Do you fear someone or something coming to take possession of something He's laid in your heart?

Remind yourself whose pastureland it is. Tell the enemy to tumble on down the road.

DAY 84

"They go from strength to strength, till each appears before God in Zion." Psalm 84:7

Your strength for today is not supposed to last you till the end of the season. It's not even supposed to last you until tomorrow. You have enough strength to get through each moment as it happens. Today.

The manna in the wilderness was given daily with just enough to last for the day. No more. No less. God tells us not to worry about tomorrow and yet we expel all of today's strength on tomorrow's problems and then wonder why we are tired. We are so scared His strength, patience, power and love will run out. We fear we may somehow use them all up and then some even bigger tragedy will happen, and we've already used all the strength and gifts He gives.

Not so.

Verse five states, "Blessed are those whose strength is in You, whose hearts are set on pilgrimage." The pilgrimage. The ever-continuing journey.

For some reason we approach this life and fallen world as if we are supposed to have all the answers, all the strengths, all the problems solved right this second. And if another fire starts up, we begin to wonder and doubt what He's already shown us.

He provides daily strength. Daily bread. Daily. Moment by moment. He does this because He's *with* you on the pilgrimage. Guys. We aren't traveling to 'get to Him." We *get* to travel *with* Him. And He provides for everything as we need it.

Where are you missing Him with you today because you're worried, He won't be with you tomorrow?

Praying you will lay down the what if burdens of tomorrow and pick up the strength for today that He provides.

DAY 85

"The Lord will indeed give what is good, and our land will yield its harvest." Psalm 85:12

Our land will yield its harvest. It will yield what has been planted. He planted love, faithfulness, righteousness and peace into us. He came, was crushed and buried and rose up out of the dirt to bloom into an eternal harvest *for us*.

It's not about what we plant. It's about what He's already done, what He's already planted.

Verses 10-11 say it clearly, "Love and faithfulness meet together; righteousness and peace kiss each other. Faithfulness springs forth from the earth and righteousness looks down from heaven."

Faithfulness comes up. Righteousness rains on it.

If your land is feeling dry urge yourself to press on. Remain faithful. His righteous rain is coming. If the sky is dark, get ready, His downpour will produce a great harvest.

What harvest are you waiting on today?

Praying He will give you patience as you continue to watch for fresh sprouts.

DAY 86

"Bring joy to Your servant, Lord, for I put my trust in You."
Psalm 86:4

Joy and trust don't always easily go together. It is hard to think joyfully in the middle of a situation requiring trust. It seems easier to let the mind wander to the outcome, all the what if's, the wonderings of God's faithfulness.

It's ok to ask for help in that type of a surrender. It's ok to ask for joy in the middle of the confusion and fear. Joy is a sign of complete trust and it's a picture of a focus on what is good and whole and not incomplete. It centers on what is true regardless of what the situation may seem. If we remember who He is and what He's already done, joy is easier to find.

Where are some areas you are needing joy in today as you trust Him? How can you hold trust and joy simultaneously?

Praying that He becomes your joy as you let go.

DAY 87

"This one and that one were born in her and the Most High Himself will establish her." Psalm 87:5

Psalm 87 is a short chapter packed with some hidden beauty. In the beginning we see a love psalm to Zion, the holy mountain where the Holy God rested. Glorious things are said of this city of God (vs. 3)

The middle verses show Him naming different regions that are not Zion or Jerusalem but saying they were born there, and He will establish them. It seems He will give them the blessing of Zion even though they aren't Zion.

None of us were born into the holy of holies. There is nothing we could have done to earn the right to be from Zion, God's chosen place. But He sees each one of us and claims us as being born in His holy land. He calls the regions by name and claims He will establish them.

Think on that. He gives you claim to something that is not yours and then explains that He will establish it, keep it, for you. It's. Not. Your. Work. It's His. It's always been His.

We get to claim we are of Zion, the holy mountain, *because He claims us.* We have the benefit of bloodline even though we're not born from it.

If you find yourself striving to earn and keep your place, know you don't have to. He claims you. He keeps you. There's nothing you can do to change that.

In what area do you find yourself striving? What would it look like for you to let go?

Praying you realize all the ways He's claimed you today.

DAY 88

"Is Your love declared in the grave, Your faithfulness in Destruction?" Psalm 88:11

The title of Psalm 88 is "The Suffering of Affliction." Not very hopeful or cheery. But oh, is it real.

No one gets through this life unscathed without affliction. We all have found ourselves in the pit without strength (vs 4). We have felt forgotten and cut off from His care (vs. 5). For some reason this is a hard or shameful thing for some to admit. To accept the fact that at times we feel God has forgotten us or stopped caring. "If He's so great why has _____ happened? Where are you now?!"

The psalmist boldly asks, "Is Your love declared in the grave, Your faithfulness in destruction?" A plea, a taunt, a sincere question. Are You here in my darkness, in this death? Can I say You have been faithful when destruction lies on either side?

It is ok to ask these things. It is ok to yell them, to feel them. You are not alone. You are not a 'bad' Christian if this is where you are. Jesus even asked, "Why have You forsaken me?" on the cross. He actually knew the plan and still asked where God went.

We don't know the full plan. God expects us to feel all the emotions, not just the Sunday Morning ones. He is big enough to hold your anger, fear, confusion, doubt. Hold it up to any sliver of light you can find. Be honest with it. It's ok to sit with it for a time.

The very beginning verse states, "Lord, You are the God who saves me; day and night I cry out to You." The psalmist knows God saves. Just like you know. Yet, he is still crying out to Him day and night. Constantly. You're not too much for Him. Your pleas, your requests, your questions. Not. Too. Much.

Do not stuff what you are feeling. Take it to Him. The good, the bad, and the ugly. Even in the deepest, darkest, pit He is still

110

there. Keep calling out, even if it's ugly.

Is there a question in your heart that you've not allowed yourself to ask?

Praying for you today to know that He is big enough for anything you have to bring Him. It doesn't scare Him or upset Him.

DAY 89

"I will sing of the Lord's great love forever; with my mouth I will make Your faithfulness known through all generations." Psalm 89:1

There is such power in music. When we use our breath to sing and remind ourselves and others of God's truth, we unlock a deeper understanding of that truth.

From early Old Testament Stories, the Israelites waged war on their enemies with their musicians in the front. The singing led them forth. It empowered. It reminded. It let the enemy know something big was coming.

It is easy to fall into the habit of only praising when things are easy and as hoped. However, it is so important and powerful to sing praises *even if* you aren't feeling it. Sing truths over yourself and others when all you can hear are the fears and the lies. If you can't sing them for yourself, ask someone else to sing them over you. Play a worship album and let the words and intentions revive you until you can sing them yourself.

Regardless of what your situation is today, His love is great, and it is forever. I encourage you to sing until you believe it.

Challenge - get still and quiet. What song comes to your mind? What truth is in it that you can claim? Can you put your own breath behind it and sing it? If not, can you think of an area in your life where He has shown Himself to be proven faithful? Can you speak it and thank Him for it?

DAY 90

May the favor of the Lord our God rest on us; establish the work of our hands for us; yes, establish the work of our hands."
Psalm 90:17

We all have a purpose, a calling. When we realize what the purpose is we frequently want to go all in towards it. We work with fervor and strive for excellence, hoping to make God proud and to fulfill what we feel we were put here to do.

That enthusiasm is a wonderful trait. For me personally, it runs out of steam and then I strive and strive to gain it back. I hustle and beat myself up until I feel like His favor is back. I try to establish myself. Futile.

However, not only does God tell us what our work is, we can ask Him for help with it. His favor will rest on us. It doesn't matter if we finish the checklist or if we hit that next goal. His favor, His approval rests on us. It doesn't yell. It doesn't push. It doesn't hurry hurry hurry. It rests. He will establish the work of our hand.

Establish usually means two things - set up and achieve permanent acceptance. It is He who sets up the work of our hands. It is He who achieves permanent acceptance for our life work, our mission, our calling.

Even your pursuit of finding your purpose is a purpose and He will establish it for you.

He wants us to set our eyes and hearts on *Him* and not a calling or a vision or a purpose. Seek Him first and all the other will be added and it will be favored and established by Him.

Sometimes we just need to focus on the purpose of the next hour or day. What is that for you today?

Praying you feel Him with you as you do your next step.

DAY 91

"He will cover you with His feathers and under His wings you will find refuge." Psalm 91:4

It is interesting that He uses a graceful, delicate symbol to represent His protection. A wing. Feathers. The picture of protection we normally visualize is one of tough and rough. Hard edges. Stern. How beautiful that within the entire chapter of Psalm 91, through all the sentences reassuring protection the psalmist uses rest, comfort, softness as the theme.

How many times have we believed we had to show a brave face before entering a trial? He tells us to find our strength in *rest*. He uses feathered wings as a blanket over us.

"His faithfulness will be your shield and rampart." (vs 4) As you face yet another shard of this broken world, think back on how He has proven faithful. Trust in that. Let that knowledge be your shield and your rest. You don't have to do anything. It is finished.

Where are you trying to put on a brave face when your strength could actually come from resting?

I pray you find refuge in the rest and comfort He provides today.

DAY 92

"They will still bear fruit in old age, they will stay fresh and green, proclaiming, "The Lord is upright." Psalm 92:14

In the forest there is a biological phenomenon that trees use known as light deprivation. Basically, the "mother tree" shades the young saplings so that they only receive about 3% of the sunlight that could be available to them. If the mother tree did not do this, the sapling would shoot up quickly and would grow tall but would be missing so much strength and tenacity. Its trunk would not be able to withstand insects eating away at its bark nor the winds it would battle high up on its own. So, the sapling grows slowly, taking decades to reach the canopy and full sunlight.

This is such a beautiful reflection of Him. Oh, how we want to shoot up and stand tall, spreading our branches, bearing our fruit. But, like saplings, some of us have been in the dark. We are not growing as quickly as we would like. We are surrounded by so many other mature trees that bask in the sun.

May this scripture and this nature picture remind you He makes all things beautiful in His time and sometimes His time takes decades because He knows you're not ready.

You will still bear fruit no matter how long it takes. You will stay fresh and green. There is no hurry. The Lord is upright. He is like the mother tree protecting you, feeding you nutrients through the roots and covering you with His canopy of branches. When He knows you are ready you, too, will shoot up, grow tall, and bear fruit.

What areas have you already experienced a slow growth?

Jot down what fruit has come from that time as a reminder to others and yourself.

Praying you see how He has protected you in the slow and darker times.

DAY 93

"Mightier than the thunder of the great waters, mightier than the breakers of the sea- the Lord God is mighty." Psalm 93:4

The ocean is a curious thing. Waves can be gentle and peaceful, or they can be thunderous and mighty. We have all seen the after effects of storms. It is easy to tell when one has been through an area. The waters demand respect, awe, fear.

So does He. His mighty waves and breakers are not to destroy you. They come and ravage anything that keeps you from Him. He doesn't just passively think about you. He mightily moves Heaven and earth for you, to rescue you, to be with you. (Psalm 18 shows a beautiful picture of this.)

Regardless of calm and peaceful or thunderous and mighty, the waves never stop. They constantly reach for the shore.

His waves of might, love, and peace are always constantly reaching for you as well. He is on your side. He is always calling out to you. Watch. Listen.

What is one way you know His waves keep coming to you?

Praying for you to feel those waves in new ways today. May your focus be bold enough to see Him in unexpected areas.

DAY 94

"For the Lord will not reject His people; He will never forsake His inheritance." Psalm 94:14

Reject - dismiss as inadequate; not to one's taste; inappropriate

God will never dismiss you. He will never see you as not enough. He will never see you as too much.

What an exhale. There is nothing you could bring to Him that He would look at you and dismiss you. There's nothing you could bring Him that He would declare not good enough. Never, in all your worries, fear, doubts, emotions, could you ever be too much for Him.

Why?

You are His.

Think of all His attributes. His glory. His might. His great agape love. All His characteristics were in the fingertips that molded you. There's no way a god that good and powerful could ever make something that would not be glorious. It's not in His nature to turn His back or walk away. He will never forsake His own inheritance. You have His fingerprints all over you. He claims you. He calls you *very* good.

Is there something heavy on your shoulders you fear talking about with Him? Maybe you think you can't because you feel it's your fault that you're in the situation that has you down? Maybe you fear He would not approve of you speaking so plainly with Him. He wants nothing to stand in the way between the two of you.

I pray you know and trust there is nothing you could bring Him that would ever, ever make Him turn away. He's for you. You are His. (Romans 8:38-39; Isaiah 43:1)

DAY 95

"In His hands are the depths of the earth, and the mountain peaks belong to Him. The sea is His, for He made it, and His hands formed the dry land." Psalm 95:4-5

God could have chosen to create the earth using only one landscape. No variety. No changes in the horizon or the atmosphere. But everywhere you look, He creates new and different things. No two flowers are the same, no two sunsets, clouds, animals, trees, people, experiences, perspectives. And just like this passage states, He holds them all. He owns them all. He made them all. These two simple verses teach several big lessons.

    1. Do not compare yourself or your experiences to anyone else's. You are unique and valuable because of your differences. Don't diminish them.

    2. Know that no matter what stage of life you are in, He is right there with you. Some of us avoid the darker emotions while some of us actually fear the good ones. Afraid of taking our eyes away from the what ifs to enjoy the moment. No matter if you are in a dry season or harvesting from the rain, He made both seasons for purpose.

    3. It is significant that the passage says He holds the depths of the earth and owns the mountain peaks. When you are at your lowest point, He is holding you. When you feel the most isolated, He is right there with you in the absence. If you are in the middle of a mountain top season, scripture says that belongs to Him. This does not mean you don't get to celebrate. Quite the opposite. It means, He's the one hosting the party so don't forget to include Him in it!

He wants to be a part of every part of your day. Your highs. Your lows. Your boring and mundane. He is an ever-present God who wants to be in relationship with You.

Do you tend to believe He is only in one area or another - the highs or the lows?

Praying you find Him wherever you are today.

DAY 96

"Let the fields be jubilant, and everything in them; let all the trees of the forest sing for joy." Psalm 96:12

It is easy to be jubilant when the harvest is ripe and abundant. It makes sense the trees would sing for joy when full of fruit. But this passage reminds us it is everything in the fields, and all the trees of the forest, regardless of if your fields are full of crops or tumbleweed, regardless of if your branches are barren or blossoming.

It is so easy to base our praise on what we see in the seasons, forgetting the character of the Creator does not change. As believers, we can be jubilant and sing for joy because despite the state of the fields, we know the One who tends the crops and tills the soil. We learn His heart through all the seasons. That heart is always towards us. It is always working for our good and His glory.

Can we sing for joy and be jubilant when the ground is dry, and the sky is clear?

May your song be joyful regardless of your seen or underground harvest today.

DAY 97

"The Lord reigns, let the earth be glad; let the distant shores rejoice." Psalm 97:1

Before man was created, God formed the earth and the shores. He called all His creations good. Scripture speaks of rocks crying out, of the earth groaning. I believe this earth, though fallen, knows its Creator as well.

One day *all* will be new. Every part of the fall will be reestablished and redeemed to its original state. The mosquitoes' bite will be no more. The rose will have no thorns. Tree pollen will not cause us allergies and humidity will be gone! (Praise!) I encourage you to think of other examples of restoration the new earth will show.

Just as we yearn for restoration, this earth does, too. Every beautiful sunrise, breeze in the tree, animals cuddling up to one another, each wave crashing on the shore is the rejoicing of creation. The earth is glad because the Lord reigns. May we join in the celebration as we eagerly await the restoration.

Can you let your imagination take control and ponder the restoration of the earth? What do you most hope for in the new heaven and new earth?

Praying for you that this exercise brings you joy and a new perspective of our Creator.

DAY 98

"The Lord has made His salvation known." Psalm 98:2

What a thought. God created. He gave us free will. He came to rescue despite our own choices that led us outside the garden, and He made known the path back to salvation. He created and continues to show us the way back in.

It's not a guessing game. It's not a "Good luck! Hope you find your way!"

Not only did He lovingly come back to rescue, redeem, and restore but He makes sure over and over and over again to point us to the path of salvation. He makes His salvation known. He gave us a choice in the Garden. He gives us a choice outside of it as well. He gives us choices daily, every hour, every moment to take steps back into an awareness of His presence.

Be still. Listen. He makes the way of salvation known. He calls to you. He sings over you. He lovingly waits for you.

Pause. What parts of you are still enslaved? What thoughts keep you captive?

Praying you see Him showing you the way to freedom in every area of your life.

DAY 99

"Lord our God, You answered them." Psalm 99:8

One of the most difficult parts of Christianity to grasp is the awe-struck holiness, wonder and might of our God coupled with the fact that time and time and time again He answers us.

It is easy to imagine a powerful being. It is not hard to imagine a close confidant. But to put the two together is difficult to understand. How can a God so powerful, so set apart, a God who could create anything He wanted at the blink of an eye still bend to hear, let alone answer?

The same God who fires the sky with passion upon your awaking, sprinkles the night sky with glitter, keeps your heart beating while you rest, also wants you to bid Him near.

He answers each of us on a personal level. Throughout scripture He chose to use different forms of communication with His children. Sometimes a whisper, sometimes a bush, sometimes a raging storm. Your language with Him is unique and won't look just like everyone else's. But know that He does answer you.

Look back over your life. Reflect on a time when you know He answered you.

I pray today these memories refresh and restore you and that your fellowship with Him sweetens as you hear Him answer you.

DAY 100

"Know that the Lord is God. It is He who made us, and we are His; we are His people, the sheep of His pasture." Psalm 100:3

There is so much goodness and comfort in this verse. This verse starts out reminding us that the one we surrender to is one who is worthy to surrender to. He is God. Big G. He's not someone who hasn't proven themselves or one who isn't sure what the next step should be. He is faithful. All knowing. Creator of all things. Including us.

He does not create and turn away. We are His. He claims us. We are the sheep of His pasture.

We are not a creation that an artist makes to sell. One that is left on a whim or made haphazardly. We are the sheep of His pasture. Sheep represent so many things in that time period. One of them is wealth. We have value to Him. You have value to Him.

He is a Great God.
He made you.
He claims you.
He values you.

Is that hard for you to comprehend? How would it change your daily life if you lived out of that belief?

I pray today you approach each situation with the confidence of knowing your value, worth and whose you are.

DAY 101

"My eyes will be on the faithful in the land, that they may dwell with me." Psalm 101:6

Where are your eyes looking? We live in a fallen world full of broken promises, broken hearts, broken people. Our expectations are not met on a regular basis. Our plans never go quite the way we envisioned. But. If we look around, there is *still good*.

My mom once drew a dark dot on a paper and asked me what I saw. I looked at her crazy and replied, "a dark dot." To which she replied, "well, yes, but you didn't mention the white all around it."

Because of the fallen world we all have dots on our papers. We could choose to focus on them, or we could put our eyes on the faithful. Choosing to look at the unstained part of the paper, does not negate the dot. If whatever you look at is your focus and whatever you look at gets bigger, then why spend energy and focus on the thing we want to diminish? Turn your eyes to the One who is more faithful than any. You will then find He's been there all along. Focus on Him. May He increase.

Where is a dark dot taking your energy? Could you spend some time today focusing on the positives?

I pray today you release control and focus on what is good knowing that won't cause everything to fall apart.

DAY 102

*"You will arise and have compassion on Zion, for it is time
to show favor to her; the appointed time has come." Psalm 102:13*

I wonder what Zion must have been feeling before the appointed
time of compassion. Forgotten? Angry? Guilty? Confused?
Abandoned?

The subtitle for this chapter is 'a prayer of an afflicted
person who has grown weak and pours out a lament before the
Lord.'

Hear me! Come quick, for my days vanish like smoke. (vs.
1-3 paraphrased) Have you ever felt that? "Lord, do you not hear
me crying out, screaming to you? Banging on this door? My days
are flying by here and yet, You are silent."

I don't know why He chooses silence as a response. Why,
if He knows our hearts, our prayers go unanswered. Why at times
prayer seems a test of our faith instead of a relationship.

What I do know is one of the most loving things about
Him is that He understands that He is hard to understand.

We do not know the appointed time, but we know there is
one. We don't know when relief, understanding, comfort will
come, but we know it's coming, and we know He is with us until
the appointed time.

We know the dark of night is not the end. It's just a sliver
of time before the silver sunrise shatters the fears and doubts. We
know the night will end. The sun will rise. The Son will rise.

I encourage you to live through the dark knowing the
morning's coming. We know how it all ends. Each trial. Each
setback. Within each hard season, day, minute the end is the same.

Jesus rises with compassion and favor for us. Again and again and again.

Is there a part of your life that feels it has been in darkness for longer than you can continue to bear?

I'm praying with you right now that the morning will come quicker than planned and until it does you will feel His presence with you through the night.

DAY 103

"He redeems your life from the pit and crowns you with love and compassion." Psalm 103:4

David knew the ins and outs of this psalm. He had literally been anointed and crowned and also been in many a pit and cave.

And so have we. We each have had seasons or moments of pit dwelling. And honestly, sometimes it's comforting there. Familiar. Easier, it seems, to accept the fall instead of climbing out.

But yet.

In one glance, we catch a quick glimpse of Him. He redeems us up out of that pit time after time. He sets our feet back on solid dry ground. How many times have you braced for impact, steadied yourself for the guilt and shame that you knew must be coming after falling into the pit yet again? "How many times do I have to tell you? When will you learn? You are so selfish!"

He says nothing like that. Instead, He raises our chins and places a crown of love and compassion on us. He continues to remind us of who He is and therefore who we are.

David later states the Lord has compassion for He knows how we are formed. He remembers that we are dust. We so quickly forget He knows every detail of us, His "very good" creation. We hide our shortcomings, ashamed feelings, afraid of the penance we assume we will have to pay. Hear this deep in your dusty bones: He *understands* what He creates. He understands you. He paid the penance himself.

The next time you find yourself in a pit, whisper His name. Let Him redeem you again and crown you with love and compassion. Let Him remind you He understands. He understands you.

Are you believing the lie that you have fallen into the pit too many times and that He's not going to rescue you this time?

I pray against that lie right now and that you know you are never too far gone, never too deep in a pit that He won't come and pull you out. Praying He reminds you of truth today.

DAY 104

"All creatures look to You to give them their food at the proper time. When you give it to them, they gather it up. When You open Your hand, they are satisfied with good things." Psalm 104:27-28

Hunger. We all experience it. Be it hunger for food or connection we all know what it's like to want deeply.

There have been many times when my children have explored the pantry looking for something to cease their hunger. More times than not they choose something that has a quick satisfaction but doesn't last. Chips, cookies, all the things we may consider 'good' things. Meanwhile, they don't realize a meal is in the oven and if they can hold on just a few minutes more their hunger will be satisfied with true good things. Things that will last and will meet their hunger needs as well as give them nutrients for a stronger and healthier body.

He knows your hunger. He understands it. He understands why you reach for the quick snack that will temporarily quiet your hunger. The snack of busy schedules, unnecessary purchases, certain relationships, gossip. I'm not sure what is in your pantry that is a common go to for you. But know that if you can allow yourself to sit with the hunger a moment longer, He has a sustaining and satisfying meal waiting for you.

He opens His hands and satisfies us with truly good things. He doesn't just throw us quick fixes to hush us up. He knows what we truly need. Maybe that prayer hasn't been answered yet because it's still cooking. He could give you the quick snack as an answer, but He knows your satisfaction would be quick lived and that hunger would come raging back.

Go into the kitchen with Him. See if you can smell the aroma of the meal He is preparing. Hints around you of what He is creating for your specific need and desire. He cares for you and the desires of your heart. He knows what you hunger for and He will not leave you starving. He satisfies with good things at just the right time.

Where in your life do you know this to be true?

I pray today you are satisfied with Him.

Day 105

"He spread out a cloud as a covering and a fire to give light at night." Psalm 105:39

In Exodus, the Israelites are led through the desert by a pillar of cloud by day and a pillar of fire by night. In their time of wandering and uncertainty, He always showed His presence.

When we are walking through uncertain terrain, unsure of where we are called to go, He will provide direction. His presence may be as a covering of clouds, foggy and thick. We may feel as if we are trying to see through dense cloud. Could it be fog is used as protection and comfort? Maybe He only wants you to see what is directly in front of you, your next right step as if you are traveling through a foggy morning only able to see a few feet in front of you. When surroundings and optional pathways are obstructed from view, it allows us to better see what is right in front of us. Maybe His fog is a protection.

Other times He leads by fire. Bright, passionate, fearful. The very oxygen that surrounded you through the fog, may be captured by a very alive fire, burning up the darkness, allowing you to see despite the absence of the sun.

It is true. He works in mysterious ways and His ways are not our ways. But just as pillars never left their place in front of the Israelites, He, too, never leaves His place by you. The absent feeling, frustration for not being able to see clearly and know all the steps of the next chapter on the first page could be His pillar of cloud guiding you one short distance at a time.

The steps that seem obvious, but fearful to take could be His pillar of fire reminding you of His presence and power in the dark of night.

Either way. He has not left you. He didn't send you to the desert for you to figure it out by yourself. He's with you every step. Guiding you by cloud and fire.

Are there times when the fog of a situation could have actually been a blessing? An uncertainty stalling you until a clearer answer is made known? Have you experienced His presence as a fire? An obvious choice, but one that is fearfully stepped into.

I pray peace for you today and that you will be able to hear Him in the confusing fog and in the scary certainty.

Day 106

"Yet He took note of their distress when He heard their cry; for their sake He remembered His covenant and out of His great love He relented." Psalm 106:44-45

New parents are amazed at how quickly they can understand the different cries of their baby. They know which cry is hunger, tired, diaper, etc.

I love how this psalm specifically states that "He took note" of their distress and cry. He knew what that cry meant. He knew the depths of it.

Just as a new parent knows what's behind the cries of their child. He, too, knows the words from your heart even if you don't.

He knows our specific cries and He remembers His covenant with us.

It does not matter if it is your first of 500th cry to Him. He takes note. He moves on your behalf. Never stop crying out. Never forget what He's done and what He's capable of still doing.

How does it feel to know that He takes note of your cry?

May you know that He knows you on such a level that He takes note of your distress and knows the cry of your heart.

Day 107

"They loathed all food and drew near the gates of death. Then they cried to the Lord in their trouble, and He saved them from their distress." Psalm 107:18-19

All throughout scripture we see the ebb and flow of humankind. One minute sinking in peril, crying out in distress, the next praising Him for His salvation and deliverance. Right back to forgetting what He's done, following old patterns and habits. Crying out in despair. On and on and on. The cycle continues.

The psalmist here describes loathing all food and drawing near to the gates of death. Sounds like they refused all help and stubbornly did their own thing, ending up right at the end of their rope.

They cried out.

He saved them.

Have you been there? Isn't it easy sometimes to sit in the darkness, chains laying open on our wrists, yet we still sit paralyzed? It's comfortable there. We know what to expect. We refuse the help offered by those around us, the food given to help sustain and nourish our soul.

Sometimes it feels the effort to receive requires too much. Sometimes we refuse the help because we think it's weak to accept it. "I can get out of this prison on my own. I'm fine."

Either way we end up nearer and nearer to the gates of death.

We either get so tired of sitting there alone or we exhaust ourselves trying to find our way out, too prideful to ask for help.

Until we cry out we've had enough. We can't take it anymore. We finally call out for the help that has been offered all along.

And He Hears us.

He saves us from distress. Time and time and time again. The cycle continues.

Hear me, friend. There is no place too far He can't bring you back. There is no darkness too dark His light won't flicker truth.

It does not matter how close to the gates of death you find yourself. Our King has defeated those gates once and for all. They have no power over Him which means they have no power over you, love.

Do not let shame, pride, or apathy keep you quiet. He has more for you. Cry out. He's ready to rescue you as many times as needed.

Tough question - Is there food/help being offered to you that you are refusing? If so, ask yourself why.

I'm praying today you learn that sometimes the strongest thing we can do is receive the strength of someone else.

Day 108

"My heart, O God, is steadfast; I will sing and make music with all my soul." Psalm 108:1

Steadfast - Resolved. Unwavering.

After my dad died, I refused to sing in worship. I thought me holding back would somehow punish God since I believed He had punished me.

Praise Him for His understanding and forgiveness of temper tantrums. There will always be seasons when you do not feel like singing, worshiping, praising. That's not what we base those actions on. We worship because no matter what our hearts feel, He remains the same. Unwaveringly so.

We must continue to worship especially in the times we don't feel it. It reminds our fickle hearts of truth. It reminds our hearts of His faithfulness.

Our hearts remain steadfast. Not always happy. Not always understanding. Steadfastly **seeking** Him.

Today I encourage you to seek Him, especially in the places you don't feel like it. I promise you He's there. Waiting for whatever small sliver you have to offer - be it confusion, anger, joy, sadness. He just wants you. Remind your heart of *His* steadfastness. Yours will follow.

Day 109

"While they curse, may You bless." Psalm 109:28

David holds nothing back in this psalm. His "friends" have turned on him. He's realized they have lied about him. In verse four he states that though they accuse him, he is a man of prayer. In which he then follows up by praying for intense detriment to fall upon his former friends. "May his days be few...May his children be fatherless...May his descendants be cut off." (Vs. 8-13) Not the prayer many of us would expect from the Bible.

David was not ashamed to express his disgust with their treatment of him. He was obviously hurt and angry. Take note of his actions. He took his anger to God. He did not shove it away and bid them blessing and not address the woundings he had suffered. He knew his worth because of Who created it, and he knew it was not ok for that worth to be treated poorly.

Today's culture seems to have two responses to this type of treatment - a refusal to stand up for oneself believing this is the turn the cheek, humble behavior Christ calls us to. Or the other extreme of going directly to the one who spews such hate and give the same treatment in return.

David shows us here the best way. He took it to the One who understood and was big enough for his big feelings. He did not ignore the unjust treatment. He knew he was a child of the King and because of that had immense worth. When we simply ignore the poor treatment of one of His creations, we are saying we don't value it enough to care for it. We don't look kindly upon another who ignores the mistreatment of animals or children. There are activists for all species. Don't you know you are worth even more than that to Him? (Matthew 10:31)

Don't ignore the mistreatment others may give you. Address it and release it to Him. Resist the urge to go back to the source of the woundings. There's no sense in trying to force them to see something they cannot. So go to the One who truly knows. Ask Him to remind you and remind them about your worth and theirs.

David knew his true worth and honor came from God alone and *not the opinion of others.* He boldly asks for God's blessing in the midst of a social curse. "Prove them wrong!" He seems to say. Because he knows who gives Truth and he knew the only way it could be proven was through Him. There was nothing he himself could do to change their opinions of him.

May your self-worth always come from the perspective of your Creator. May you know your worth enough to know when someone is disgracing it and respect yourself enough to know Who to go to about it. Address it and release it with God. Let Him take care of the rest. You are whole in Him.

Day 110

"Sit at my right hand until I make your enemies a footstool for your feet.' The Lord will extend your mighty scepter from Zion, saying, 'Rule in the midst of your enemies! "Psalm 110:1-2

The beginning words are spoken from God to Jesus. Sit. While I make your enemies your footstool. If Jesus is told to sit and be still - what makes you think you must get up and do the heavy lifting all by yourself? Jesus trusts God is taking care of His enemies. He is taking care of yours, too. Can you sit down today and allow Him to care for you? The worrying, the striving, the rule worshiping - what would it look like to hand it over to Him? It would leave you able to truly see Him in this world as He fights for you. Let Him.

The second half of this passage says so much in three little words - 'in the midst.' It does not say to rule your enemies once they are defeated, but in the middle of them. Your enemies may not be coming after you with sharp weapons trying to invade your physical territory. Your enemies may be the one who said something that got back to you and you can't figure out how to forgive. The person you can't trust. The lies you regularly hear that tell you you aren't enough. Those are your enemies. But He says to rule in the midst of those enemies. While they are cold, show them warmth. While they ooze self-doubt, show up with confidence. When they tell you, you aren't enough - remind them of Who says differently.

Lean in and listen to what He's called you to rule over. What kingdom is yours? Your household? Your students? Where you are in location and influence is a part of the Kingdom He has entrusted to you. Do not let your enemies keep you from showing His character, to your Kingdom. Even though people may not understand you, may not respect you - it doesn't change your identity in Him. You are His child. One He fights for. If He is on your side - who could ever be against you? (Romans 8:31)

Will you allow yourself to take that exhale now? Here in this moment. In the middle of the schedule, the children fighting, the bills, the enemies.

You can produce His fruits and rule your kingdom even among the unknown diagnosis, the worry of tomorrow. He is asking you to sit and let Him bring those worries under your feet as a footstool. He is asking you to remember that you rule in the midst of those enemies, not just when they are defeated.

Day 111

"Great are the works of the Lord, they are pondered by all who delight in them." Psalm 111:2

Many people know God's works are great, impeccable, incomprehensible. They stop there. They notice, they awe, but they don't care to ponder on them. For some His works are so hard to understand it keeps some people from even trying to ponder them. Some take it a step further and seem to shame anyone who may question the intricacies of His works. "Don't ask questions. Just trust."

This verse teaches it is ok to ponder, to wonder, to question His great works. The Creator gave us that ability to question. To wonder. To ponder.

He is there in the questioning.

The magnitude of this universe is too great for us to fully understand. The intricate goings on of the protons and neutrons in every cell. The creatures of the deep that no one has even discovered yet, He sees them and knows their scientific classification.

He knows what babies dream of. And why some people love cilantro, and some think it tastes like soap. He knows why specific Chopin nocturnes can take me back 15 years in an instant.

There is not a question you could ask that He hasn't already thought of.

The psalmist says those who ponder are delighted by His works. Not vengeful, not shameful, not disrespectful.

Don't be scared to lean into the questions and wonderings. Not one person knows the complete answers to all the ponderings. But He wants you to seek Him.

Yes, trust Him with the answers, but also trust that He's big enough for any and all of your ponderings.

"Doubt is not the opposite of faith - certainty is." - Anne Lamont

What about God and this creation makes you ponder?

I pray today you allow yourself to ask and that He gives you answers.

Day 112

"They have no fear of bad news, their hearts are steadfast trusting in the Lord. Their hearts are secure, they will have no fear, in the end they will look in triumph on their foes." Psalm 112:7-8

They will have no fear of bad news. Is that even a thing? No fear of the bottom falling out? Waiting to hear results of a test? Sending your kid off to drive alone for the first time? This world gives us plenty of reasons to fear bad news.

And it's true, He does not promise us a life full of only the good things. Bad things are around the corner for us all. Yet.

It *is* possible to not fear what tomorrow may hold simply because you know Who will be there with you. We spend so much time hoping, pleading, working, begging Him to ensure a guarantee of no bad news. We fret. We wring our hands. We 'what if' and plan ahead in prevention mode. We try to control.

But what if we spent that energy realizing our hearts can be steadfast because of our Loving Creator who has promised to never leave us? "If He is for us, who could be against us?" (Romans 8:31) Paul goes on to list a litany of bad news and states that none of those things will ever separate us from Christ.

"In the end they will look in triumph on their foes." Can we look in triumph *if there are no foes?*

I urge you to imagine your absolute worst-case scenario. Now, can you see yourself looking triumphantly upon it? This is what He wants you to understand. Your weakness brings out His strength. If you can't imagine yourself defeating the biggest fear, imagine Him. His strength lies within you.   I

It's time to take back our present moment from all our anxieties of the future. It is time for us to enjoy the peaceful moments of no news instead of giving it away to fear of what ifs.

That is how you triumph. That is how you begin to live a life abundantly. Keep your eyes on Him.

Psalm 113

"He raises the poor from the dust and lifts the needy from the ash heap; He seats them with princes, with the princes of His people." Psalm 113:7-8

Throughout scripture God is proclaiming the theme of these verses. Through every story from Adam's to yours today He offers *more*. There is more than just lifting us from the dust and ash heap. It was more than just rescuing Moses from infant death, the Israelites from slavery, three young men from a furnace. He rescued and offered abundance. Moses moved from the reeds to the royal palace to the ruler of a nation. The Israelites moved from bondage to the promised land. Shadrach, Meshach and Abednego walked out of a fire and into a promotion. The end goal is never to just be saved from death, but to LIVE abundantly *with Him right now.*

God wants more for you than just to save you. He never delivers us and leaves us. He lifts us from the dust and places us next to Him. He saves us from hell so that we can be with Him. Not just so we won't do 'bad things.' It's never been about what we do or don't do.

It's always been about what He has already done for us. The story does not end at the cross, it begins with His footprints walking out of the grave.

If you are in the dust and ash heap, call out to Him. He stoops low to come and raise you up. But remember, He doesn't just dust you off and leave you be. He places His best robe around you, calls you His and seats you next to Him.

Where are you living among the dust? Where are you dust free, but not truly with Him?

May we all be aware of the abundance He offers with His presence. May we all remember it's more than being dust free. May we all seek and find His presence abundantly waiting for us in each moment.

Day 114

"Who turned the rock into a pool; the hard rock into springs of water." Psalm 114:8

There is nothing too difficult that God cannot use for you. The psalmist takes the reader back to the memory of the Israelites leaving Egypt and wandering in the desert. Even though their own choices led them to 40 years wandering away from comforts and promises, God still allowed the arid and dry rock to transform into a life-giving substance for them.

The beginning of this chapter refers to large natural creations trembling, breaking, moving because of the presence of God. He ends by showing how God comes down to the small, onto a personal level. A small rock, broken for His people.

The God of the shaking mountains, the parting waters is also the God who sees you where you are. Your 'small' worries and needs. Your personal, secret trials. He will use the very things that cause us harm to break open and refresh us.

What is causing you harm today?

Ask Him to turn it into something to bring life.

Day 115

"May the Lord cause you to flourish." Psalm 115:14

Flourish - grow or develop in a healthy or vigorous way, especially as the result of a particularly favorable environment.

Psalm 115 is in a set of psalms sung during Passover called the Hallel Psalms and were sung by Jesus on the night of His crucifixion. While Jesus was carrying the cross, these words were fresh off His lips just hours before. "May the Lord cause you to flourish." Those looking on would not consider His situation one of a favorable environment, would not consider this moment as one that is flourishing.

The beginning of this psalm states, "Not to us, O Lord, not to us, but to Your name give glory." Jesus pleaded with the Father to not have to drink of this cup. To not have to climb the hill, endure the whips, die on the cross. But, in order for God's plan to come into fulfilment, His great glory of redemption, He must go through the unthinkable.

When we trust Him and not ourselves, we can sing as Jesus did on the night of His death, "May the Lord cause you to flourish." We can look at our current circumstances of distraught, pain, loneliness, and know despite those situations He will cause us to flourish.

Jesus made it so that we all have a chance to flourish, to grow healthy. It makes the words He said that night even more profound. "May the Lord cause you to flourish," He said as He was fulfilling the very thing that would allow us to do just that.

Where are you flourishing right now? Thank Him for it. Where could you use more growth? Ask Him for steps to get there.

Praying you find yourself flourishing today. Growing in health and reconciliation.

Day 116

"Return to your rest, my soul, for the Lord has been good to you. For You, Lord, have delivered me from death, my eyes from tears, my feet from stumbling that I may walk before the Lord in the land of the living." Psalm 116:7-9

The beginning of this chapter begins with "I love the Lord, because He heard my voice; He heard my cry for mercy." The psalmist can state his soul can return to rest in verse seven because of the very fact he knows the Lord has heard him. This shows the enormity of God's love for us. He hears us when we call for help. He turns His ear to give attention. Because of that we can return to our rest.

The version of the word rest used in this verse is one of plural form meaning total and complete rest.

How many times have we struggled through or feared a specific situation, prayed over it, but after it was dealt with in one way or another, we went right back to fretting over it? Giving our energy to something not worthy of it.

God does not want you to prove yourself to Him. He is not waiting on you to prove you have a certain amount of scripture memorized or given away enough money. He hears you. He has been and will continue to be good to you. Your soul can let go. You can rest. Completely.

Trust that whatever is weighing on you today can be completely surrendered to Him. Call out to Him. He knows your specific voice and cares for you.

Trust Him and return to your rest.

Where are you finding yourself only catnapping and not really resting?

Praying you will be able to trust Him and rest in His truth. He cares for you. He cares about the situation that has you concerned. Let Him handle it while you rest.

Day 117

"For great is His love toward us and the faithfulness of the Lord endures forever." Psalm 117:2

With only two verses, Psalm 117 is the shortest chapter in the Bible. "Praise the Lord, all you nations; extol Him, all you peoples. For great is His love toward us, and the faithfulness of the Lord endures forever. Praise the Lord."

Short and to the point. Sometimes we don't need any other direction than to just praise Him because His love toward us is great and His faithfulness lasts forever.

In the anger, confusion, joy, mundane - Praise the Lord because He loves you and will never leave you. He is faithful.

How can you apply that sentence to your current situation? Don't dismiss what you're going through, just look at it through the lens of Psalm 117:2.

Praise because He loves and is faithful.

Day 118

"I will give You thanks, for You answered me; You have become my salvation." Psalm 118:21

"You have become my salvation."

Become my salvation. It's a process. As cool as it would be to be introduced to Jesus and immediately know all the secret things, that's just not how it works. The Creator took His time with the creation of the universe. Jesus took 30 years to even begin His ministry. The best things don't come immediately. The growth happens in the waiting.

Philippians 2:12-13 tells us to work out our salvation with fear and trembling for it is God who works in us in order to fulfill His good purpose.

Salvation always has been and always will be on His shoulders. Not ours. That's the point. Our job cannot be to save ourselves. We respond and we keep responding. Every day. Every moment.

Salvation, relationship, it's an ongoing process. Salvation is not a one-time event at the end of an aisle at vacation Bible school. It keeps happening.

We are not in a linear relationship with Our Father. We don't back slide and then do an about face to see Him again. It's continual. It's cyclical.

On the peaceful days when all is well - He becomes our salvation.

On the days where things seem to be changing every hour - He becomes our salvation.

Dropping off your kid at college, saying goodbye to a loved one, anger rising from your core at Him - He becomes our salvation.

You keep calling out to Him. He will answer. He will continue to become your salvation.

How does the idea of salvation being an ongoing process resonate with you? Yes, you have been secured for Heaven since the beginning of your relationship, but the idea of salvation being a process means there's always more to discover. There's always more to be redeemed because we still live in a broken world.

I pray today you will be aware of other areas that need more redemption, more salvation. I pray you won't see that as a chastisement, but as an opportunity to become more intimate with Him.

Day 119

"Your hands made me and formed me; give me understanding to learn Your commands." Psalm 119:73

One thing is for certain, the Bible can be a confusing book. There are times it seems to contradict itself. For instance, the command to not kill, yet there are many stories of war set in action by God.

If I'm being honest, it is hard for me to know when the line of grace and compassion ends and the law of being noble, righteous and holy begins. How do we accept all people, but also state that sometimes they have to change?

I fall on the line of grace and acceptance and letting the rules slide. I was a rule follower, no... a rule worshiper for many many years. And then I broke so many and ran into His grace.

I understand when we truly meet His grace, we will be urged to desire more of Him and therefore will be pricked when we begin to live in a way that distances ourselves from Him.

This verse brings me much comfort because it shows it's not a mind reading game with God. He knows how He made you. Some of us are black and white, some move more toward the gray line. We don't have to guess and hope we are right. If we need clarification with His commands, all we have to do is ask Him.

Do not shirk back afraid He will be angry or roll HIs eyes because you just don't get it yet. That's a human reaction. He will impart understanding on you if you ask for it. Be still. Listen.

What commands has He given that you need help understanding?

Praying He will give you more answers today.

Day 120

"Save me Lord from lying lips and from deceitful tongues."
Psalm 120:2

I'm a firm believer in the power of words. Words we say to others. Words said to us. Words we tell ourselves. The psalmist asks God to save them from lying lips.

When we come into agreement with lies and deceit, it causes massive destruction. Lies imprison. Truth sets free. We must take every thought captive. Comments said to us need to be held up against the truth of what He says about us.

Once we accept a lie and allow it to take up residence in our thought life, it continues to worm its way into as many nooks and crannies as possible. Things you have believed about yourself or others since childhood have taken up permanent residence in your life and therefore affect how you interact with the world. It really becomes a vicious cycle and is one reason this verse is so powerful.

Save us, Lord, from believing the lies. Save us from falling for deceit. Let us find the root of the lie and break agreements with it so in turn we stop living from the lie. Give us truth. Set us free.

What lies have taken up residence within your thought life? How does it affect your interactions with those around you?

Praying you recognize the lies and that you find the courage to ask Him to save you from them. I pray truth and freedom for you in every area right now.

Day 121

"He will not let your foot slip. He who watches over you will not slumber; indeed, He who watches over Israel will neither slumber nor sleep." Psalm 121:3-4

We are a people who want to be able to do it all on our own. I remember when we brought our first child home from the hospital. Eva Grace was a NICU baby and after 9 days in the hospital we finally got to welcome her home. I will never forget being so afraid to fall asleep because I knew it would be the first time in her life where she wasn't hooked up to machines and there would be no watchful eyes looking over her. As I fought sleep with everything I had in me, I repeatedly asked Jesus to watch over her while we slept.

And of course, He did.

If I would have kept trying to fight sleep in order to keep a watchful eye on her I would have ended up doing much more harm than good. I had to surrender my inabilities and limitations because He has none.

And just as our daughter did not go unseen that night, neither have you.

It may be a first season for you in a new place, without watchful eyes and systems in place helping you immediately know when something has gone awry.

Know that you can rest your eyes. He doesn't slumber. He will not send you out unguarded or unprotected.

Where do you fight relinquishing control?

May you trust His watchful, caring, attentive eye. Quit peeking. Go back to sleep. He's got this.

Day 122

"May there be peace within your walls and security within your citadels. For the sake of my family and friends, I will say, 'Peace be within you.'" Psalm 122:7-8

David is asking for peace to be in the holy land, Jerusalem. The temple was not yet built, but he knew the importance of peace and security within a set apart place. A place set aside for worship and reconnection with the Father, be that a temple, church building, or city.

As shown in verse eight, David also shows the importance of peace *within the people of that place*. "For the sake of my family and friends, I will say, "Peace be within you."

Peace within a place. Peace within the people. You can't have one without the other. If a place is restless, the people will be as well. If a person is restless, they affect the place around them.

If we look at this verse on the other side of Jesus' resurrection, we know that we are now both - the people and the temple (place.) Because of the torn curtain, His temple is now in us. We are the people and the place.

Is there something that is keeping you from peace right now? It could be your surrounding or it could be within.

How are your surroundings affecting your peace? It may be as simple as tidying up or getting a change of scenery.

How are you affecting your surroundings? Are others able to exhale in your presence?

What is it that has a grip on your peace?

I pray for both your surroundings and your spirit. I pray for the peace that passes all understanding will guard your heart and your mind today. (Phil 4:7)

Day 123

"So, our eyes look to the Lord our God, till He shows us His mercy." Psalm 123:2

Upon first reading of this verse, it would be easy to think, "If God is so great then why would His mercy take so long to appear?"

The question could also be, if God is so great, why would He even begin to glance at us with mercy? If He is pure and holy, how and why would He choose to look upon us?

I don't fully know, but He does.

We will never understand the why, but we fight to choose to believe He does. And when it seems wrath is all around us, we choose to focus and keep our eyes on the Lord until mercy comes.

I think of Peter. He looked to Jesus while he sank in those waves. And even though Jesus' hand was there, Peter still began to sink. I'm sure Jesus reached out before Peter really knew he was sinking, but I have to believe there was a split second of panic and pleading for mercy as Peter readjusted his focus from the chaos and fear to the merciful hand waiting for him. Sometimes, I wonder if we keep calling out for mercy without knowing it's already there. His hand is just hard to see among the waves.

Are you waiting for mercy in a situation? Keep looking. His hand is extended. He may not stop the storm, but He'll pull you up out of the water.

He delights in showing mercy.

Day 124

"The snare has been broken and we have escaped." Psalm
124:7

The snare has been broken. Freedom.

You can escape. You can escape the burdensome life of fear and striving. The stifling life that says it all depends on you. That you are chained because of what you've done, and you have to be the one to find freedom. You have to be strong enough, good enough, even tempered enough to break the snare that enslaves you.

False. The snare has already been broken.

"If the Lord had not been on our side...the raging waters would have swept us away." (vs. 3-5)   The whole battle of this life is recognizing three things - the snare, the One who has broken it, and the freedom that awaits us.

Lies try to tell us how to free ourselves, but just like the Chinese torture toy, it only locks us further down. Look to Him for your freedom. Look to Jesus to break your snare. It's already finished. He's waiting for you.

Where are you keeping yourself imprisoned when He has already declared freedom? Can you claim that freedom for yourself today?

Jesus, please allow us to breathe in the freedom you give us. Thank you for breaking the snare. Now show us we can escape.

Day 125

"Those who trust in the Lord are like Mt. Zion, which cannot be shaken, but endures forever." Psalm 125:1

Mt. Zion is significant for many reasons in scripture. It is a real place and a spiritual symbol representing eternity. Its physical location has shifted numerous times, but all these years later, it is still standing and will continue to. I'm not sure why God chose that physical location to hold such importance, but He chose it. So, it will never be shaken.

He also chose YOU.

Israel has seen its fair share of tumultuous times. Yet, it still remains as a physical location and as a spiritual symbol.

Just like Mt. Zion, when we trust in the Lord and what He has said and done, we will remain standing. Psalm 125 says Mt. Zion cannot even be shaken, let alone fallen.

Also, just like Mt. Zion, you will encounter your fair share of tumultuous times and many changes. Yet when you trust in God and His astounding love, mercy, faithfulness and strength you, too, will not be shaken. You will remain.

Mt. Zion is known to be a City of God and you are also a Temple of the Father.

It's not on your shoulders to keep your mountain tall and secure. It's on you to trust that He will.

When you trust in Him, you will be able to endure anything.

Where are you afraid your mountain will crumble?

I pray today you will be as Mt. Zion, unshaken and trusting in the Lord.

Day 126

"Our mouths were filled with laughter, our tongues with songs of joy. Then it was said among the nations, "The Lord has done great things for them." Psalm 126:2

There seems to be this notion that in order to be holy, you must be somber at all times.

Aren't we so glad this isn't true? Can you just imagine the sound of Jesus' full on belly laughter? Can you imagine the children being children and making His eyes crinkle with pure joy?

He does that over you as well. He smiles with happy eyes. You bring Him joy. You do not have to hide your happiness and joy from Him. Just as parents love to see their children enjoy a gift, God delights in seeing you be delighted.

He is there for us in sorrow and in difficulty, but do not forget His presence in the middle of a grab your side, can't catch your breath, full bodied laugh either. He is humorous. It's not sinful to meditate on that part of His character.

Can you think of a moment you just know He had to be laughing alongside you?

May you sense Him in the delight you find today.

Day 127

"Unless the Lord builds the house, the builders labor in vain. Unless the Lord watches over the city, the guards stand watch in vain." Psalm 127:1

From the beginning of Creation, God has extended a hand to us to partner with Him. He created animals; Adam was asked to name them. God created plants; Adam tended to them. He does not want us to just be an observer, but a participant. How compelling. What an honor.

We must be careful to not forget it is a partnership and not a sole task. We may toil and labor doing what we believe He has called us to do, but if we do not partner with Him and invite Him into it, the work will be in vain.

You are a friend, an heir. You are not a slave sent to do His bidding.

You are a partner, not just a spectator built only to applaud Him from the stands.

May you know the completion, not of a task well done, but of partnering with the One who set it all in motion.

What can you invite Him into today?

Today I pray you find the courage to invite Him into the task at hand. I pray you have the discernment to hear His wisdom and the courage to accept His hand.

Day 128

"You will eat the fruit of your labor; blessings and prosperity will be yours." Psalm 128:2

Just as Psalm 127 teaches of partnering with God in the work, Psalm 128 proclaims the receiving of the fruit of the labor.

It is ok for you to enjoy the fruits of your labor be that financially or time wise. God did not create us just to watch us toil away and not experience the joy and product of the work. And He sure didn't call for us to deny the goodness of a creation.

If we partner with Him to create what He has called us to form, it is not bragging to enjoy it.

Part of the job of a parent is to teach the importance and joy of hard work. How cruel would it be to make my kids work and save money for a new gadget and then deny them excitement upon receiving and playing with it?

Where can you allow yourself to enjoy the fruit of your labor?

Jesus, thank you that you made a world that operates with sowing and harvest, labor and fruit. May we not deny either part of the process.

Day 129

"They have greatly oppressed me from youth, but they have not gained the victory over me." Psalm 129:2

Psalm 129 is another Psalm of the Ascents sung by Jews on their way to a festival. Commentary states that they sing it not as a song of triumph but of survival.

The psalmist says, "They have greatly oppressed me from youth." Possibly meaning the oppression is ongoing. It's still something they deal with. Because we live in a fallen world, we will experience oppression.

This psalm of survival reminds us, just like yesterday and the day before, God will see us through despite the oppression around us. It may continue, but it will not be the victor.

Maybe our job is not to defeat certain things, but to continue to bring them to Him and allow Him to do what He does - bring freedom and abundance where strongholds try to chain and destroy. That sounds like victory to me.

Are you feeling continually oppressed? Can you proclaim that this situation will not steal your victory?

May your strongholds not keep you from lifting your face today. May you understand that sometimes it is a lifelong struggle, but it doesn't mean you end in defeat. It ends with victory.

Day 130

"Israel, put Your hope in the Lord, for with the Lord is unfailing love and with Him is full redemption." Psalm 130:7

Israel - the one who wrestles with God; Israel - all of us.

While we wrestle, while we wait, continue to put your hope in Him. The psalmist understands the difficulty of trials. This walk with God is not free from despair. It is not a ticket to a carefree life. Quite the opposite. When we decide to hope in the Lord, to turn to Him, we are simply admitting there is a choice. A choice to either look at the darkness or look at the light. When we look at the light, we will find our hope. It doesn't negate the difficulty of what we are going through. It simply reminds us He is there. Regardless of the outcome of our situation His love will not fail us. If the absolute worst thing happens - He remains. Regardless of what you choose to focus on, His love remains. He offers full redemption.

We should never dismiss the difficulty of what we or others are going through. Life is hard. Jesus says so Himself. (John 16:33) The beauty of Christ is that He provides hope, relief, love in the midst of the suffering.

We don't try to work to rid ourselves of suffering. We rest to receive Him *while* we suffer.

What may be keeping you from putting your hope in the Lord?

May the Lord remind you of times when He has been faithful. May those times give you more confidence to hope in Him today.

Day 131

"I do not concern myself with great matters or things too wonderful for me. But I have calmed myself, I am like a weaned child with its mother; like a weaned child, I am content." Psalm 131:1-2

If you've ever been around someone who expected you to read their mind, this verse should be very uplifting for you.

David acknowledges here that there are things that he just cannot understand. Matters too great for him to grasp. However, he goes on to say he has calmed himself. He is content. This is because David knows the Lord does not expect us to read His mind and understand all of Him. We can't.

God knows His ways are not our ways. I would imagine it grieves Him to see His children trying to figure it all out on their own. Which direction to go. The answer to an age-old question. How to love the one person who is just so hard to love.

God does not send us out empty handed and tell us to figure it out. He's not waiting on us to read His mind and do His bidding. In fact, for us to assume we could even do so is mighty big headed of us. Verse 1 states, "My heart is not proud, Lord, my eyes are not haughty." Of *course*, we can't figure it out. Of course, we don't have all the answers. He doesn't expect us to read His mind, because He knows it's legitimately impossible and we are prideful to think we ever could.

David finishes one of the shortest chapters in the Bible by reminding Israel to simply put their hope in the Lord. That's all He wants of us.

When things get difficult, we don't go looking for answers and then turn to Him. We turn to Him for the answers.

Where might you be concerning yourself with matters that are too wonderful for you to understand?

May you know today that He is not expecting you to figure that out. He wants you to invite Him in to help you.

Day 132

"I will bless her with abundant provisions; her poor I will satisfy with food." Psalm 132:15

Today's Psalm speaks of a resting place for the Lord. It mentions how David sought for the perfect place for the Lord's temple. In verse 13 the Lord chooses Zion as His dwelling and proclaims in verse 15 He will bless her with abundant provisions and will satisfy with food.

Because of Holy Spirit, *we* now are Zion. He has chosen you as His dwelling. And because of this you will be blessed with abundant provisions.

I love the second half of the verse, "I will satisfy with food." He does not just throw us a bone. It is not just a nibble. If we allow Him, He will satisfy completely.

Trust that He dwells within you. Know that He will fill His dwelling with good things. There is abundance. There is satisfaction. It just may not be where you are currently looking. Take Him all your longing. All your needs. All your joys. He's there. He provides. He satisfies.

Can you think of yourself as Zion, His dwelling place? How do you think the Lord cares for His dwelling place? Is He one to show neglect or does He show honor to a place that holds His presence?

I pray that idea fills you with the joy of being a child of God today as you trust that He cares for you and all your needs.

174

Day 133

"[unity] is like precious oil poured on the head, running down on the beard, running down on Aaron's beard, down on the collar of his robe." Psalm 133:2

What an image. How does it relate to unity though? Doesn't oil poured on the head represent a blessing for that person?

David proclaims how good and pleasant it is when God's people live together in unity (verse 1). And then describes oil running down priest Aaron's head, beard, and collar. Oil represents anointing and greeting. As one entered another house, sometimes oil would be offered as a refreshment.

Anointing Aaron specifically is important as he was the high priest. Unity is not just good for individuals; it is good for the collective group. If the high priest, the leader, is anointed then those blessings will spill over onto the people just as that oil spilled over past Aaron's head.

I also love the connection of oil being a greeting and refreshment. When we are united, each caring about one another and not just self, we all are refreshed, and that refreshment benefits us all.

May you feel united in a family, community, kingdom of God today. May you be a refreshment to others as they are to you.

Day 134

"Praise the Lord, all you servants of the Lord who minister by night in the house of the Lord." Psalm 134:1

Who minister by night in the house of the Lord. Proof that ministry is not always sunshine. And by ministry I don't just mean working for a church.

As many times as you have done a selfless act for someone there will always be a voice that says you've not done enough.

As many times as you have prayed for a healing there will always be a disease incurable.

Ministry and darkness sometimes go together. Many times, they go together. But we are to praise Him regardless. Because we know darkness is never the ending. It loses its power when the praise happens despite the hardship.

This is not something that comes easy to people. It is not just a gift some have, and others don't. It is a practice. And sometimes you may have to praise through tears and gritted teeth.

It's not that you dismiss the dark. You just don't give it the final say.

As I write on the other side of multiple traumas and dark dark seasons I can say to you I know how hard it is to praise during such times. The benefit of having gone through those trials is that I can tell you they do end. Not at all how you might think. Probably not always how you would like, but you will get through them.

He does not ask us to praise Him because He needs it. He asks us because we do. We need the reminders of what is true, especially during the darkest nights of our soul.

Praise Him all you servants who minister by night in the house of the Lord.

He is closer than you can see.

Praying for you today.

Day 135

"For the Lord has chosen Jacob to be His own, Israel to be His treasured possession." Psalm 135:4

Treasured possession. Treasured. Held dear. Favorite.

That's you.

Let that sink in. The Lord chooses you, pursues you and you are a treasured possession of His. The things that concern you, those things concern Him. The things that make you smile. He smiles, too.

Verse 6 states, "The Lord does whatever pleases Him." It pleases Him to choose you to be His own. He doesn't do it out of guilt or coercion. He doesn't have to. It's not because you earned it or because you are qualified. He is pleased to choose you. And He keeps choosing you. All He asks of you is to choose Him.

That is what we praise. That's what all of this is about. Knowing He chose you and you respond by choosing Him.

Ponder His choosing of you. Can you decide today to choose Him specifically and intentionally today?

Holy Spirit, please show them today how you have specifically chosen them as Your own.

Day 136

"With a mighty hand and an outstretched arm; His love endures forever." Psalm 136:12

There is nothing that keeps you from Him. No sickness. No bad day. No bad attitude. No distraction could make Him withdraw His arm from you. Nothing is too heavy for Him to hold.

His love endures - presses on - fights through - forever.

You are never too far gone, never too 'bad'. That one thing you've kept hidden too afraid to tell anyone. The one secret that you most fear being exposed. His strong hand still reaches out to you. It doesn't scare Him. He's not ashamed.

Do not let anything be hidden from His love. He wants all of you to bask in His warmth.

What is keeping you from being fully present with Him?

I pray you take time today to reach out. Hide nothing from Him. He's safe.

Day 137

"How can we sing songs of the Lord while in a foreign land?" Psalm 137:4

Sometimes, some days, the songs just aren't there.

The Israelites had been captured by Babylonians. They wept there not because of the cruelty done to them in this foreign land, but because they missed their home land. They missed the way things were. The peace of the promised land and the goodness they saw there. They longed for what once was.

I'm sure we've all felt that, especially during the 2020 pandemic. Missing the way things were. Longing for community in our homeland. And sometimes, it's just not possible to grin and bear it.

After my daddy died, I could not and would not sing in worship for a long long time. I just couldn't do it. Like the Israelites, my songs were not performances, they were utterances of my heart. And sometimes all our hearts can utter are groanings and mumblings.

What the psalmist did not know then was Romans 8:26-27. When we don't have the words, the songs, Holy Spirit intercedes for us through groans of His own.

The next time you have a season of not being able to sing the joyful songs of the Lord, know He understands. He hears the utterances of your heart, the longing, the aching. And He is interceding for you.

I challenge you today to do what I couldn't many years ago and sing through the anger and hurt. Even if it's not words, but groans. Turn your tired achy heart toward Him and see it still toward you.

Day 138

"Though I walk in the midst of trouble, You preserve my life. You stretch out Your hand against the anger of my foes, with Your right hand You save me. Psalm 138:7

Though I walk in the midst of trouble. You will walk in the midst of troubles. No matter how much good you do. No matter how many hours you pray or how much money you give. You will have trouble.

However, He saves you in the midst. He is with you among the troubles. He does not leave you alone. Verse six states that though He is exalted, He looks kindly on the lowly.

There is this notion that puts us in power and us in charge and says as long as we do x,y, and z that will secure us from all troubled paths. That is one of the biggest lies of humankind. The truth is even though life is still hard, His presence never leaves. You are not alone. Ever.

Are you walking amidst trouble today?

I pray today you sense His outstretched hand against your enemies, and you sense His right hand protecting you.

Day 139

"I praise You because I am fearfully and wonderfully made."
Psalm 139:14

You are wonderfully made. His works, His creations are wonderful. Humans are the only creation He called VERY good. That's you.

Fearfully in Hebrew means with heart-felt interest and respect. He respects His creation of you. He has a heart invested interest in You. Please remind yourself of that the next time lies shout negativity about you, His creation.

If the Creator respects you, shouldn't you also respect yourself? Do you think you know better than Him how you should be created?

Use this verse to combat thoughts of insecurity and self-deprecation.

You are a wonderful creation. If you are struggling to believe that right now, could you praise Him for something about you right now?

Jesus, may your sons and daughters see something unique about your creation of them today. May they replace an old lie of inadequacy with truth of your creation today. Show them they are very good.

Day 140

"The arrogant...have set traps along my path." Psalm 140:5

Psalm 139 speaks of how well the Lord knows us. Our inmost thoughts and our paths are always in His sight. Many of us experience hardship or trouble and immediately begin to think we are not doing what we should be doing. We misheard Him somewhere and should've chosen differently in one way or another.

Sometimes, that's true. Sometimes, as in David's case for Psalm 140, we are on the right path, but there are traps along the way.

What do we do then? When we know we heard Him correctly and we are doing as we should, but things are stuck. Things are painful. David tells us we can say to the Lord, "You are my God. Hear my cry for mercy, my strong deliverer, my shield." (verses 6-7 paraphrased.)

He's not disappointed in you for being trapped or stuck. He knows that the arrogant lay traps and evildoers devise plans to trip up our feet. Do not hide those frustrations from Him. Tell Him and then remind yourself of who He is and His character. The Lord secures justice and upholds the causes of the needy. The upright will live in His presence. (verses 12-13)

Are you in a situation where you know you are on the right path, but there seem to be traps everywhere? Maybe you're not sure if you're on the right path and there are traps set by the enemy or if you are actually on the wrong path. That can be very frustrating and confusing.

I pray today that God shows you clearly the way to go, the path to take and that if you are on a path with enemy laid traps, He will guide you around them and release them from you.

Day 141

"May the lifting up of my hands be like the evening sacrifice." Psalm 141:2

It was customary to offer incense to God every morning and evening. David wrote this psalm at a time when he was unable to perform these rituals. He substituted the lifting of his hands in place of the evening sacrifice. He offered his heart's surrender instead.

David was likely frightened. He urgently called to the Lord. He pled for justice. It would reason that he was willing to do whatever was needed to offer the traditional sacrifices to God in order to have His protection. And David, the man after God's own heart, knew that God's protection would not come from customs and rituals. He turned his heart and hands to the Father, symbolizing the original meaning of the ritual and surrendered. *David knew that God had always just wanted his heart.*

He did not wring his hands due to his circumstances. He did not depend on his own actions to ensure his needs were met. He let go of his fear and worry. He stopped trying to control and allowed God to do what only God can.

Where might you be clinging to control? Maybe you are trusting in a tradition or a ritual to secure the answer you are longing for.

My prayer for you is that you learn the beauty of lifting your hands. Release control. There's not a specific set of actions that unlock His approval to grant your request. He just wants your heart. Turn to Him. See His face. God's character is to love and protect his children. May you deeply understand that today.

Day 142

"When my spirit grows faint within me, it is You who watch over my way." Psalm 142:3

Psalm 142 is another one of David's prayers from a cave. Hiding. Scared. Honest.

We see him first admit he is faint, weak. He cries out to God asking for help. He admits he can't do it on his own and in doing so maybe his heart shifts to the understanding that God never expected him to do so in the first place.

David was called from a young age to be the king of a nation and now he's hiding in a cave...again. But he is admitting his weakness and acknowledging that it is God that watches over his path. It always had been.

So often we feel called by God and then think we are supposed to go on without Him helping. As if we think He just gives us orders and waits for us to fulfill the plan. As if we even could! We have a kind God. We have a God that calls us and then watches over and walks with us along the way. Our God is not surprised when we hide in our cave. He is in there with us. When our spirits grow faint. He watches over our way. He is our refuge even in the cave.

No matter your situation, He is with you. He does not expect you to make it to your calling or even through the day on your own.

You are not a burden.

Is your spirit faint? Did you start with the best of intentions and now you are weary?

May you know He is still with you in your day. He does not sleep. He watches over you and will renew your strength. Call out to Him now.

Day 143

"Lord, hear my prayer, listen to my cry for mercy; in Your faithfulness and righteousness come to my relief." Psalm 143:1

There are many times we feel as though God isn't listening. We beg and plead and there's no response. Verse seven states, "Answer me quickly, Lord; my spirit fails. Do not hide your face from me." I love the confidence David has in saying that to Him. Answer me quickly. There is no formality to it. There doesn't have to be because it's a personal relationship.

The times when you feel He's not listening - tell Him. Ask Him to answer you quickly. Our frankness is not off-putting to Him. He already knows our thoughts anyway. He knows what it's like to be human and feel distance, fear and anger.

We can also know and trust that while we may be upset at His silence, we know He will answer in His time because of His faithfulness and righteousness. It is not in His character to play games with us and give us the silent treatment. He is big enough for your frustration with His seemingly silent response.

Do you feel as if He doesn't hear you right now? Remember His character. He is faithful. He will come to your relief.

Jesus, may we trust You even when we cannot hear Your voice. We know, Holy Spirit, that You will never leave us, and You will come to our relief.

Day 144

"Praise be to the Lord my Rock, who trains my hands for war, my fingers for battle." Psalm 144:1

He trains our hands and our fingers. And yet we find ourselves fighting the lie that says we must do it all on our own. He equips us each step. He cares about our hands (the big picture) and He cares about our fingers (the details.)

Can you see? He does not leave us to fend for ourselves. You are not too much for Him.

He cares about what bothers you. He trains you on how to deal with this life even down to your details.

Don't ever listen to the lie that says whatever is on your heart is not a big enough problem for Him to care about. Think of how nimble fingers must be in a war holding the weapons and defending the body. He cares down to the smallest detail. He makes all things work together for His glory.

I challenge you today to ask for help with a small detail. Watch for Him to give it attention.

Day 145

"You open Your hand and satisfy the desires of every living thing." Psalm 145:16

I used to think that I had to hide my desires from God. That I shouldn't long for anything because I had Him. Shame and guilt kept me from showing Him that part of my soul.

"He doesn't care about the desires of my heart." What a lie. What. a. lie. He cares about the desires of your heart *and* He wants to be the one to give them to you.

Just as a parent loves to give good gifts to their child, so does the Lord love to be the giver of your favorite things. Big and Small. A simple laugh. A paid bill. A front porch with a swing. A job. A friend.

Seek Him. The satisfaction of your desires is in His hand. Talk to Him, not so He can know about it (He already does,) but so you'll know He knows. And when that desire is met, you'll know it came from His open hand.

What are you desiring today? A moment of quiet or a tangible thing. Know that He will open His hand and meet your needs and desires.

Day 146

"The Lord sets prisoners free, the Lord gives sight to the blind." Psalm 146:7-8

God remains faithful forever. His goodness knows no end. You can trust Him to set you free, to help you see. To restore to you what was lost.

Where do you feel you are living in the dark? What has you imprisoned? What lie continues to control you and your thoughts? Are you in the prison of always fearing the worst? Always striving for your worth? Does your prison master continuously taunt you with "you're not good enough?"

"He upholds the cause of the oppressed and gives food to the hungry. The Lord sets prisoners free, the Lord gives sight to the blind, the Lord lifts up those who are bowed down." (verses 7-8)

You are not alone. You are not too much for Him. You are more than enough. Let Him restore your sight to truth. Let Him set you free from what has imprisoned you.

Are you living in freedom right now? Are you seeing, truly seeing? Are you blinded by continual lies that imprison you?

I pray now that you will feel the heaviness of broken chains on your wrists and that you feel tired from keeping your eyes shut. When you feel these things may they remind you the chains are broken, and you can be free from what weighs you down. Your eyes can look around you and He will show you great and wondrous things you could not see before.

•

Day 147

"He heals the brokenhearted and binds up their wounds. He determines the number of the stars and calls them each by name. Great is our Lord and mighty in power; His understanding has no limit." Psalm 147:3-5

I long for our viewpoint of God to change. The paradigm that says He is all-knowing and therefore impersonal and beyond our reach is simply not true. He draws close, close enough to bind up our wounds.

Verse two states that He gathers the outcasts. When others exclude you, He gathers you to Him and heals your broken heart.

His understanding has no limit. No limit. The one secret you've never told anyone for fear of being exiled - He understands. He understands why you are the way that you are. He made you.

There is nothing you could do that He wouldn't understand. Jesus came as God in human flesh so that He could understand all of humanity. The Monday woes. The complexities of relationships. The exhale when our heads finally hit the pillow. He understands. Any emotion you've experienced...He has, too. May that sink in and bring you comfort.

What does it mean to you to know that you have a God that draws close and understands? Are there places where you could invite Him closer?

I pray today He binds your broken heart, even the smallest of shards you didn't realize were broken.

Day 148

"And He has raised up for His people a horn, the praise of all His faithful servants of Israel, the people close to His heart." Psalm 148:14

Chapter 148 begins to close the book of Psalms with a decree to all things. Praise the Lord. From the heavens to the sea creatures. Wild animals to kings of earth. Young men and women, old men and children. His name alone is exalted.

Yet the last verse states that one who is to be exalted actually raises a horn (strength) for His people. Hard to grasp, yes? The One we exalt reaches down and gives us strength.

This is why we praise Him. For His goodness. For though He is powerful enough to be a ruling tyrant, a distant King, He brings us close to His heart. And that is one of the many, many reasons we praise Him.

Hallelu Yah

May His nearness be your strength today.

Day 149

"May the praise of God be in their mouths and a double-edged sword in their hands." Psalm 149:6

At first glance the ending of this chapter could be confusing and lend itself to visions of a tyrant king. Verses stating inflicting vengeance and punishment.

But look at the weapon He gives us to use - praise. "May the praise be in our mouths and be a double-edged sword."

We look back at the many chapters of David crying out in agony, asking to be released from his prison or cave. What did he always come back to? Praising the Lord. Because God proved time and time again that He is faithful. While we may not see the prison doors swing open yet, we know they will. And so, we praise even in the midst of the war. We know the praise will be the vengeance and punishment of our enemy. Our praise will bind the kings with fetters. When we use the double edge sword of praise, we reclaim our freedom from the lies that try to imprison us. We proclaim truth. And truth sets us free.

How can you use praise as your weapon and defense today?

May God's truths be our praise and may they fight off the enemy's arrows of lies.

Day 150

"Let everything that has breath praise the Lord." Psalm 150:6

Everything that has breath, praise Him.

Humans, trees, animals, the wind. May we all praise Him. With trumpet, dancing, clash of cymbals. However you express praise. Do it.

It is His breath that is in you. Allow it to work in you the way He designed it. Let your day to day unfurling of your one and only true self be a song of praise to our Lord who is as close as the air we breathe.

As you take in. As you give back. Praise.
As you inhale. As you exhale. Praise

Praise the Lord.

PSALM STORIES

PSALM STORIES

Acknowledgements

This book has been a group effort. I am so honored and grateful to have so many people that have supported and believed in me.

Emily P. Freeman and Hope*Writers - so grateful that you listened to His call and created a group for all who have a message to share. (Which is all of us, even you.)

Heather Medley - You will never know the impact our one-hour meetings in cozy rooms have had on my life. There would be no "Psalm Stories" without you. Thank you for showing me how to live in freedom.

Amanda McWhirter - I am so glad He orchestrated our meeting. From cover design to being one of my biggest cheerleaders - my thanks overflows to you. Thank you for rooting for me, friend. Now it's your turn!

Bellwether - I'm not sure how to articulate the gratitude I have for you. When my life shattered, you were there. You filled a void in a new way and became a family I didn't know was possible.

My fight club - For hours spent listening to my spirals, for spontaneous trips and hangouts, for helping me to find fun again - I love you forever sisters.

Meg - Your story inspired so many of the ones written here. Your faithfulness in His faithfulness has birthed a witness of His love. It's one of my biggest honors to witness it.

The Duners, the Dunnahs, the Framily - you were the first ones to help me see I had something to share. Your encouragement and support helped to get me here. I am forever grateful for our framily.

My sissy - We are strong women who have been through many a fire. Here we are on the other side. So grateful He gave me you as my protector and encourager. You help me believe in myself like no other.

Eva Grace and Isaac - You are the absolute best gift anyone could ever ask for. It is one of my most honored roles to be your mama. I pray these words carry through to you and your children and you learn how very much He loves you and wants to commune with you every day.

My favorite - It's you. Our vows still remain true. You complete everything I'm not and you polish everything I am. You are the clearest picture of His character. I'm forever grateful for all of the lies you've helped me to replace with truth. Thank you for believing in me. I love you mani mani.

My El Roi, Jesus - Thank you for seeing me. Your patience and Your faithfulness continue to astound me. You are the reason. You are the freedom. You are the abundant life. I'm so grateful You share it with me. May I see You more. I love you.

ABOUT THE AUTHOR

Liz Petty is an author and teacher. Her passions include crafting words, creating beauty, teaching music, and leading worship. Liz loves finding the meaning in the mundane and the symbolic in the simple. She longs for each person she encounters to know Jesus and know the abundant life to which He calls each of us. Liz lives in Rome, Ga with her elementary school sweetheart, Josh and their two children Eva Grace and Isaac. Read more at lizpetty.net and on social media (Liz Petty fb; @lizpetty431 ig),

Made in the USA
Columbia, SC
09 May 2021